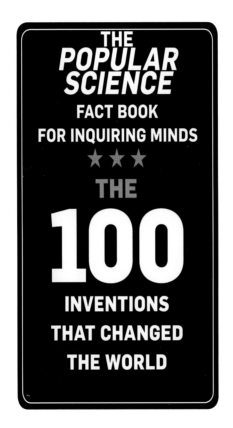

THE
POPULAR
SCIENCE

FACT BOOK
FOR INQUIRING MINDS

★ ★ ★

THE

100

INVENTIONS

THAT CHANGED

THE WORLD

THE
*POPULAR
SCIENCE*
FACT BOOK
FOR INQUIRING MINDS
★ ★ ★
THE

100

INVENTIONS
THAT CHANGED
THE WORLD

Edited by
Matthew Elkin

Cavendish
Square

New York

This edition published in 2018 by Cavendish Square Publishing, LLC
243 5th Avenue, Suite 136, New York, NY 10016

First Edition

Website: cavendishsq.com

This publication represents the opinions and views of the author based on his or her personal experience, knowledge, and research. The information in this book serves as a general guide only. The author and publisher have used their best efforts in preparing this book and disclaim liability rising directly or indirectly from the use and application of this book.

All websites were available and accurate when this book was sent to press.

Cataloging-in-Publication Data

Names: Elkin, Matthew/ editor.
Title: The 100 Inventions that changed the world / Matthew Elkin.
Description: New York : Cavendish Square, 2018. | Series: The popular science fact book for inquiring minds| Includes bibliographical references and index.
Identifiers: ISBN 9781502632913 (library bound)
Subjects: LCSH: Inventions—History—Juvenile literature. Inventions—Miscellaneas—Juvenile literature.
Classification: LCC T48.E45 2018 | DDC 600—dc23

Editorial Director: David McNamara
Editor: Michael Sciandra
Associate Art Director: Amy Greenan
Production Coordinator: Karol Szymczuk

PHOTO CREDITS
Images from: Andreas Trepte; Associated Press; Azcolvin429; Benjamin P. Horton; Caltech, NASA; Charlie Watson (USAID/Rainforest Alliance Forestry Enterprises); CIA; Damien Jemison/LLNL; DARPA; Dr. Mridula Srinivasan, NOAA/NMFS/OST/AMD; Dreamstime; ESO/A. Roquette; FermiBubble-NASA's Goddard Space Flight Center; Frank DeLeo, National Institute of Allergy and Infectious Diseases (NIAID); Frettie; Greg Sanders/USFWS H. G. Wells, Julian Huxley, G. P. Wells; Istock; J. Hester and P. Scowen (ASU), NASA; Library of Congress; Mandy Lindeberg, NOAA/NMFS/AKFSC; NASA; NASA/SkyWorks Digital; NASA_DOE_Fermi LAT Collaboration; X-ray, NASA_CXC_SAO; Infrared, NASA_JPL-Caltech; Optical, MPIA, Calar Alto, O. Krause et al. and DSS; NASA_JPL-Caltech_STScI_CXC_ SAO' NASA_JPL-Caltech.jpg; NASA-Ames-JPL-Caltech; NASA-CXC-M. Weiss NASA-Jim Yunge; NASA-JPL-Caltech-STScI; NASA-JPL-Caltech-UCLA; NASA-Pat Rawling; NASA, ESA, J. Hester, A. Lollcrabmosaic; NASA, ESA, M. J. Jee and H. Ford et al. (Johns Hopkins Univ.); NASA; ESA; G. Illingworth, D. Magee, and P. Oesch, University of California, Santa Cruz; R. Bouwens, Leiden University; and the HUDF09 Team; NASA/ ESA/JHU/R.Sankrit & W.Blair; NASA/JPL-Caltech; NASA/JPL; NASA/Pat Rawlings, SAIC; NASA/Peter Reid, The University of Edinburgh; National Institute of Allergy and Infectious Diseases (NIAID/NOAA) Pavel Riha; Shutterstock; Steffen Richter, Harvard University; Thinkstock; Thomas Schultz; U.S. Fish and Wildlife Service

22MEDIAWORKS (www.22mediaworks.com)
President Lary Rosenblatt
Designer Fabia Wargin Design
Editor Susan Elkin
Writers Charles Piddock, Susan Taylor, Susan Elkin,
Bonnie McCarthy
Copy-editor Laurie Lieb
Photo Researcher David Paul

Many thanks to Amy Bauman and Kevin Broccoli for editorial support.

Printed in the United States of America

Contents

Fiber Optics

Jeans

Pasteurization

Kevlar

Telegraph &
Morse Code

Remote Control
& Alternating Current

Automobile

Steam Engine

Fertilizer

Sewing Machine

Cotton Gin

Cloning

Radio

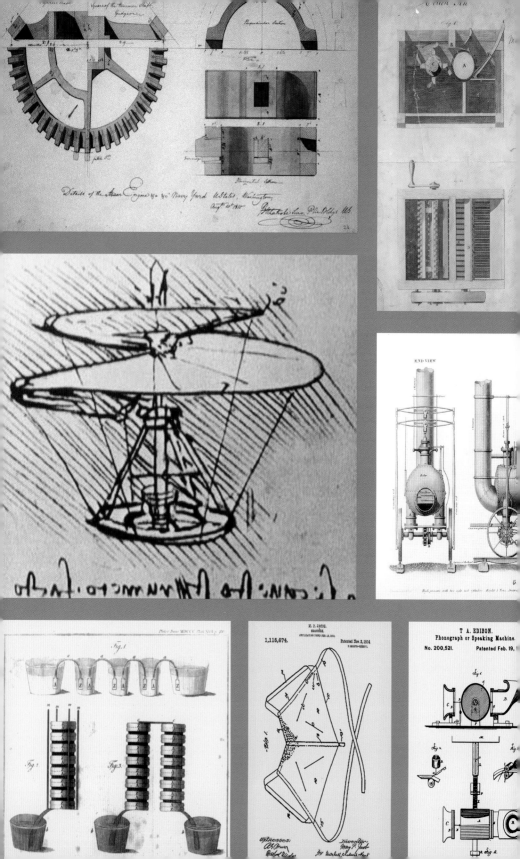

Introduction

Steve Jobs, co-founder of Apple and one of the greatest innovators of our time, once said, "Creativity is just connecting things. When you ask creative people how they did something, they feel a little guilty because they didn't really do it, they just saw something. It seemed obvious to them after a while. That's because they were able to connect experiences they've had and synthesize new things."

Jobs knew what he was talking about. History's greatest innovators stand on the shoulders of those who have come before. Using discoveries that were hard-won or accidentally uncovered, inventors have changed the way we live by working passionately to connect the dots and make sense of the world around us.

Today, the modern people of innovation continue to analyze past technology in pursuit of the advancements that will define our future. Where will computers go from here? How can we leverage progress with the needs of an increasingly globalized community, and what will trigger the next medical breakthrough? These and many more unanswered questions continue to inspire some of the greatest minds of our time.

The inventions on the following pages illustrate the courage, resilience, and innovation of the human spirit, while simultaneously suggesting the challenges that remain. Perhaps, most importantly, the advancements listed here also demonstrate how a single spark of brilliance can touch us all. Writer William Arthur Ward once said, "If you can imagine it, you can achieve it." All these inventions began in someone's imagination, but it is their achievement that truly changed the world.

OPPOSITE: Great inventions can come about by accident—a burst of information or slow, plodding experimentation—but all at some point must be fleshed out on paper if the promise of their potential is to be fulfilled and duplicated for the future. Examples of some of those drawings include (clockwise from top left) Watt's steam engine, Whitney's cotton gin, Stephenson's locomotive engine, Edison's phonograph, Jacob's brassiere, Volta's battery, and da Vinci's helicopter.

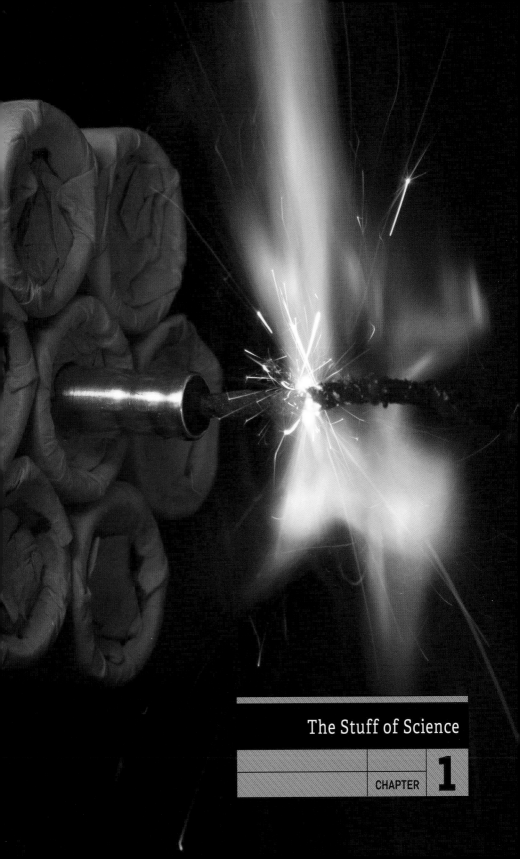

The Stuff of Science

CHAPTER 1

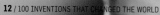

A closeup shot of Velcro's loops (left) and hooks (right).

Velcro

Many artificial objects were inspired by something organic or found in nature. Velcro, sometimes called "the zipperless zipper," is one of those items, modeled after the common seed case of a plant.

Velcro consists of two surfaces: one made up of tiny hooks and the other composed of tiny loops. When the two sides are pressed together, the hundreds of hooks latch onto the tiny loops, producing a firm binding that is easy to undo by pulling on the top surface, making a familiar rasping sound. Today Velcro is used in hundreds of products, from coats to children's shoes, blood pressure gauges to airplane flotation devices.

The idea for Velcro came unexpectedly. In 1948, George de Mestral, a Swiss engineer, went hiking in the woods with his dog. Both he and the dog came home covered with burrs that had stuck to them during their walk. Suddenly, an idea occurred to him: Could what made the burrs stick on clothes have commercial use as a fastener? Studying a burr under a microscope, he discovered that it was covered with tiny

hooks, which had allowed many of the burrs to grab onto clothes and fur that brushed up against the plants as he and his dog passed by.

Armed with this idea, de Mestral spent the next eight years developing a product he called Velcro, a combination of the words "velvet" and "crochet." He obtained a patent on his hook-and-loop technology in 1955 and named his company Velcro. Few people took de Mestral's invention seriously at first, but it caught on, particularly after NASA used Velcro for a number of space flights and experiments. In the 1960s, Apollo astronauts used Velcro to secure all types of devices in their space capsule for easy retrieval. Starting in 1968, shoe companies like Puma, Adidas, and Reebok integrated Velcro straps into children's shoes.

A 1984 interview between television talk-show host David Letterman and Velcro's US director of industrial sales ended with Letterman, wearing a suit made of Velcro, launching himself off a trampoline and onto a wall covered in Velcro, sticking to it. This widely publicized stunt furthered the craze, resulting in more companies adapting Velcro into their products.

Gunpowder

Legend has it that Chinese scientists searching for the elixir of life experimented with potassium nitrate, sulfur, and charcoal, causing an explosion that had very little to do with immortality. The emperor was entertained on his birthday with a reenactment of the experiment, marking possibly the world's first fireworks display. Colorful explosions using gunpowder, of course, still mark special occasions today. But the explosive substance also has a dark past, and the use of gunpowder in war has changed the course of history more than any other weapon.

The first wartime record of gunpowder is found in a Chinese military manual produced in 1044 C.E. On the battlefield, the Sung Dynasty used gunpowder against the Mongols to make flaming arrows. Those early battles used the new substance as a fire-producing compound that propelled flames across enemy lines. Later, crude bamboo rifles emerged.

Fearful that the technology would fall into the hands of enemies, the government forbade the sale of gunpowder to foreigners, and it remained in Chinese possession until the thirteenth century. It probably arrived in Europe by the Silk Road, and the English and French quickly developed the new tool to use in simple cannons during the Hundred Years' War (1337–1453). The Ottoman Turks also successfully broke down the walls of Constantinople using gunpowder.

When the handgun appeared in 1450, operating as a miniature cannon, each soldier was issued his own weapon. The infantry was born, and with it the modern army. All thanks to this simple, ancient powder.

The foggy beginnings of gunpowder lie deep in a Chinese alchemist's laboratory.

I intend to leave after my death a large fund for the promotion of the peace idea, but I am skeptical as to its results.

— ALFRED NOBEL

Dynamite

For Swedish chemist and prolific inventor Alfred Nobel, explosives were the family business. But they would also prove the source of one of his greatest inventions and the foundation of a global legacy.

While studying chemistry and engineering in Paris, Nobel met Italian chemist Ascanio Sobrero, the inventor of nitroglycerin (the highly unstable liquid explosive containing glycerin), nitric acid, and sulfuric acid. The substance was considered too dangerous to have any practical application, but Nobel and his family recognized its tremendous potential and began using it in their factories.

After his studies and travel to the United States, Nobel returned home to work in his family's explosive factories in Sweden. In 1864, Alfred's younger brother Emil, along with several others, was killed in an explosion at one of the plants. Nobel was devastated by the loss and determined to create a safer version of nitroglycerin.

In 1867, the scientist discovered that mixing nitroglycerin with diatomaceous earth (a soft, porous, sedimentary deposit of fossilized remains) created a stable paste that could be sculpted into short sticks. Nobel envisioned the product being used by mining companies to blast through rock. He patented his invention the same year, calling it "dynamite," from the Greek word *dynamis,* meaning "power." The new explosives transformed the mining, construction, and demolition industries. It allowed railroad companies to safely blast through mountains to lay track, opening up new avenues for exploration and commerce. Nobel became a very rich man.

It soon became apparent, however, that the same explosive force used to conquer mountains could be equally effective in decimating enemy troops. Although its inventor self-identified as a pacifist, military regiments began using dynamite in combat—indeed, cannons loaded with dynamite were used in the Spanish-American War.

Nobel was determined that his legacy would not be rooted in destruction. In his will, written in Paris on November 27, 1895, he specified that most of his estate should be used to fund prizes in physics, chemistry, physiology or medicine, literature, and peace, and be awarded to "those who, during the preceding year, shall have conferred the greatest benefit on mankind." After his death in 1896, the equivalent of what would be about $250 million today was used to establish his foundation, and the first Nobel prizes were bestowed in 1901. Today, it is this legacy that continues to inspire the world.

Teflon

Teflon is the brand name for a polymer, also called a synthetic resin. It is extremely slippery, doesn't react with water, and maintains its integrity when exposed to high temperatures.

Roy Plunkett, a chemist working for the DuPont Company in 1938, was trying to make a better refrigerator by combining a gas (tetrafluoroethylene) with hydrochloric acid. Not quite ready to combine the gas with the acid, he cooled and pressurized the gas in canisters overnight. When he returned the next day, the canisters were empty yet still weighed the same as the night before. What had happened to the gas? Plunkett cut the canisters in half and discovered that the gas had turned to a solid, creating a very slick surface in the canisters. The slippery solid was polytetrafluoroethylene, or PTFE.

The new substance, now trademarked Teflon, found multiple uses in the US war effort during World War II. It was even used in the Manhattan Project, the top-secret US program to build the first atomic bomb.

> Some inventions, such as television and stainless steel, are developed with a purpose: The invention itself is the goal. Other inventions, however, have come about completely by accident. Some inventors are looking to invent or experiment with something else entirely when they stumble upon something unexpected but useful. Teflon is one of those unanticipated discoveries.

Neither Plunkett nor anyone else at the time thought that Teflon would be of use to consumers. Yet in 1948, French engineer Marc Gregoire, after using Teflon on his fishing tackle to prevent tangling, listened to his wife's suggestion that the nonstick substance would be ideal for coating cooking utensils. Gregoire introduced "tefal" pans, the first to be lined with Teflon. In the United States, Teflon-coated pans went on sale in 1961. Today, of course, Teflon pans are in nearly every kitchen. Other applications for Teflon include building materials, space suits, computer chips, and insulating seals.

In recent years, Teflon has come under fire. As researchers delve further into the connection between modern chemicals and disease, some have linked Teflon to known carcinogens. Conclusive results are elusive, however.

Fertilizer

We live in a world of plenty. So much food is produced today that in some regions farmers are paid to not plant crops. But we haven't always understood how to make plants grow.

The last great agricultural disaster was in 1816. Freezing temperatures throughout the year left crops destroyed. Many people in Western Europe and parts of North America went hungry. German chemist Justus von Liebig was a child during this time. That experience influenced Liebig profoundly, and he embarked on a career that led to a new discipline—organic chemistry—and the transformation of the agricultural industry.

In the 1840s, Liebig's study of plant nutrition and his discovery of nitrogen (and its plant-based form, nitrate) as a key to plant growth led to his nitrogen-based fertilizer and earned him the "father of fertilizer" moniker. Of course, his wasn't the only name linked to the development of fertilizer. Agriculture is a 10,000-year-old tradition, and even in its earliest days, farmers used wood ash and manure to increase their crop yields. Gypsum, a mineral found in sedimentary rock in Earth's crust, also was and still is used, providing sulfur for plant nutrition.

In 1900, German chemist Fritz Haber developed a process to synthesize nitrogen, plentiful in the air, into its plant-based form. He used high temperatures to combine hydrogen (derived from methane) with atmospheric nitrogen, creating ammonia, a building block of economically viable fertilizer. (Haber would win the Nobel Prize for his "Haber Process" in 1918.)

The Industrial Revolution had ushered in great demographic changes, and as more and more people moved from rural areas to cities, it became clear that food production would need to be massive and steady. The first fertilizer-manufacturing plant opened in Germany in 1913. At the same time that fertilizer production began on an industrial scale, munitions factories started capitalizing on the product's combustive nature to make bombs. Throughout the first and second world wars, nitrogen-fertilizer production became big business.

Nitrogen fertilizer production is a double-edged sword. Although it is responsible for about a third of our current food production, we pay a price for our reliance on it. The use of nitrogen-based fertilizer has had a profound effect on our environment. Runoff from crops destroys river and sea life, and the amount of energy needed to produce nitrogen fertilizer contributes to climate change, as do the greenhouse gases given off in the process.

Furthermore, fertilizer manufacturing plants are dangerous places to work: plant explosions, while not common (there have only been 17 plant explosions since 1921), can cause high death tolls.

However, as Earth's population continues to expand, there is a need to move away from a reliance on oil for energy. Corn ethanol, an alternative energy source, means we'll grow more corn than ever before, ensuring that fertilizer production will remain a viable industry.

Silicone

It is difficult to find a product in use today that does not contain silicone—from glass to automobiles to electrical insulation.

In 1901, British scientist F. S. Kipping produced a synthetic polymer (a molecular structure consisting of a large number of similar molecules artificially bonded together) that had remarkable qualities. It did not conduct heat, did not react with its environment, was not poisonous, and repelled water. It also did not react with other compounds and it could be made into a rubber or a plastic solid. Its chemical name, however, was a quite a mouthful: "polydiphenylsiloxane." Kipping gave it the simpler name "silicone," and a soon-to-be indispensable ingredient of modern life was born.

Because of its high heat resistance, lubricating qualities, and non-stick characteristics, silicone has multiple uses. It provides insulation in the electrical industry, seals gaskets in the automobile and aircraft industries, and functions as coatings in textiles and papers. Dry cleaners even use liquid silicone as a cleaning solvent and satellites are lined with silicone to protect their components from shock and heat. In other industries, silicone often comes in handy as a sealant for watertight containers and plumbing pipes.

In the medical field, silicone pops up in implants, catheters, contact lenses, bandages, and teeth-impression molds in dentistry. Cookware for kitchens is often coated with silicone due to its non-stick properties. You can also find silicone in a number of personal-care items, including shampoos and shaving cream.

Look around a room and name anything you see. Chances are silicone is part of its makeup, resulting in a better product.

Plastic

Plastic is such a common part of our daily lives that it's easy to forget it is an invention of the recent past.

Plastics are not found in nature—they're man-made, consisting mainly of the element carbon found in petroleum. While most of the planet's petroleum is refined into combustible fuels, a fair amount is turned into plastic resin pellets. These pellets are made by combining short chains of carbon molecules, called monomers, into larger chains, called polymers. The pellets then go to processing plants where they are further chemically altered to make different types of plastics.

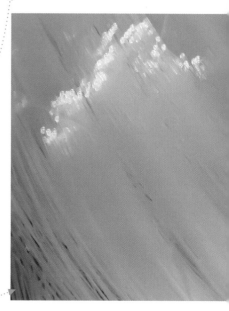

In 1909, a Belgian-born chemist by the name of Leo Baekeland synthesized the first truly man-made polymer from a mixture of phenol and formaldehyde. The condensation reaction between these monomers resulted in rigid, three-dimensional polymers, creating a substance that could be molded when hot into hard shapes. Called Bakelite after its inventor and considered the first commercial plastic, it was widely used for handles on flatware, phones, auto parts, furniture, and even jewelry.

In the 1930s, Wallace Carothers, a chemist for the DuPont chemical company, invented a polymer that could be stretched out into strong fibers, like silk. This plastic became known as nylon. Nylon is lightweight, strong, and durable. It is now used for clothing, tents, luggage, rope, and many more everyday items.

The use of these early polymers became widespread after World War II and continues today. They were followed by the creation of many other plastics, like Dacron, Styrofoam, polystyrene, polyethylene, and vinyl.

IT'S DIFFICULT TODAY TO FIND SOMETHING THAT IS NOT MADE, AT LEAST IN PART, FROM PLASTIC. EVERYTHING FROM THE CLOTHES WE WEAR

Although plastic, with its myriad uses and applications, seems like a miracle substance, it has created a large problem. Because plastic doesn't react chemically with most other substances, it doesn't decay. Instead, it stays in the environment for decades; scientists predict it could hang around for centuries. The disposal of plastic has thus become a difficult and significant environmental problem. Today, efforts to recycle plastic are being expanded in the hopes that we will someday be able to dispose of plastics more efficiently and with less harm to our world.

TO TV REMOTE BUTTONS, COMPUTER KEYBOARDS, FOOD WRAPPINGS, AND EVEN MAJOR PARTS OF AUTOMOBILES CONTAIN PLASTIC.

Carbon Nanotubes

Unlike the emperor's new clothes, carbon nanotubes, the almost invisible hollow carbon threads that possess kinetic, conductive, and optic properties, really do exist. You just can't see them with the naked eye—or even the average microscope.

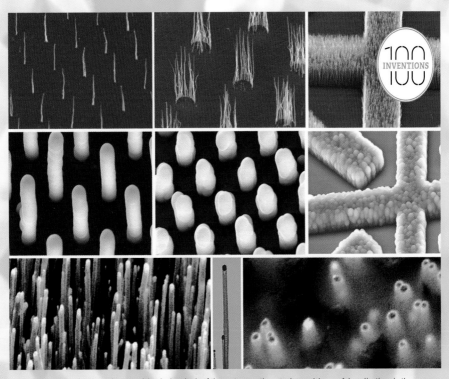

Carbon nanotubes have the potential to be hundreds of times stronger than steel, promising useful applications in the construction, automobile, and aerospace industries.

The prefix "nano" means "billionth," and a nanotube is one-billionth of a meter in diameter—approximately one-ten-thousandth of the thickness of a human hair. The experts at Nanocyl, a company specializing in these incredibly small carbon building blocks, liken its molecular structure to a tube of rolled-up chicken wire with a continuous, unbroken hexagonal mesh wall.

The most widely used process for creating nanotubes is called chemical vapor deposition, which is considered to produce the ultimate carbon fiber. This process "grows" the fibers by introducing a process gas (such as ammonia, hydrogen, or nitrogen), and a carbon-containing gas to a substrate prepared with a layer of heated metal catalysts (such as nickel, cobalt, or iron). Most scientists agree they are in the nascent stages of developing both the applications of nanotubes and the technology used to create them.

But already, nanotubes can be found in such everyday items as skin-care products that can be absorbed without leaving residue and ultra-lightweight tennis rackets that are stronger than steel. According to Nanocyl, potential and existing applications for nanotubes include use in conductive plastics, structural composite materials, flat-panel displays, gas storage, anti-fouling paint, micro- and nano-electrics, radar-absorbing coating, technical textiles, ultra-capacitors, atomic force microscope tips, batteries with extended lifetimes, biosensors for harmful gases, and extra-strong fibers.

The race for the advancement in nanotube technology is on. As nanotechnologists refine production processes and explore the capabilities of the material, the potential for inclusion in everything from the mundane to the lifesaving is limited only by our imagination—kind of like the emperor's clothes.

Spreading Ideas

CHAPTER **2**

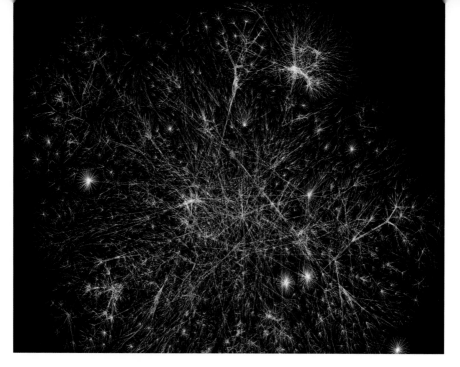

Internet

The first description of the internet came from computer scientist J.C.R. Licklider, who described a "galactic network" for sharing information. Since then, the internet has changed from a simple data-sharing device used only by government officials and scientists to a network that most people around the world rely on every day.

During the Cold War years (1947–1991), America was caught up in an intellectual arms race with the Soviet Union. Fearful that society's main source of communication, the telephone, might be targeted, the government urged scientists and universities to establish an alternative system of communication that would allow computers to interact with each other.

At the time, computers were room-sized devices that worked at sluggish speeds.

In 1969, the internet's predecessor, the Arpanet, sent the first message from a computer at the University of California, Los Angeles, to one at Stanford University in Palo Alto. The message "login" was only a partial success, since the computer crashed immediately after it was received. As technology

improved, universities and organizations developed isolated networks, but the complicated systems made connections between networks difficult. American engineer Vinton Cerf solved the problem in the late 1970s using the Transition Control Protocol, today known as TCP/IP. This new protocol allowed all networks to participate in a virtual handshake.

For most of the 1980s, the internet existed purely as a way for scientists and organizations to send data to other computers. But in 1991, Tim Berners-Lee, a British scientist and computer programmer from Conseil Européen pour la Recherche Nucléaire (the European Organization for Nuclear Research, or CERN) established the World Wide Web (WWW), a web of information that everyone could access. As the web grew more user-friendly and diverse, Berners-Lee's creation allowed all people to share limitless information, and the Internet Age was born.

During the 2012 London Olympics opening ceremonies, Tim Berners-Lee celebrated worldwide internet access when he used Twitter to send out a message—"This is for everyone"—that reached a billion people.

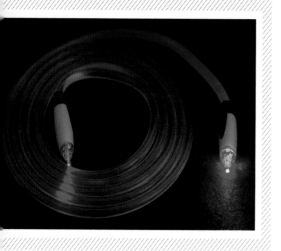

Fiber Optics

More! Bigger! Faster! Our appetite for information and the speed with which we transmit it is constantly growing. Fiber optics have transformed telecommunication by functioning as a stronger, less expensive, low-power alternative to copper wire.

Before the invention of fiber optics, scientists struggled for many years to make light travel farther without losing intensity. Finally in 1966, a Chinese PhD student named Charles Kao discovered that certain properties of glass could transfer light and energy for long distances, opening the door to the field of fiber optics. After Kao's discovery, researchers at Corning Glass Works created the first practical application for fiber optics, ushering in the great age of information. Endoscopes—tools used to see inside the human body—were one of the first objects to feature the new technology, providing detailed imaging in hard-to-reach places. Surgeons soon began using fiber optics to perform types of laser surgery, since probing in remote or hazardous locations requires extreme care.

Fiber optics have also changed communication significantly, connecting people who are separated by long distances. A far cry from Alexander Graham Bell's original telephone cables, fiber optics are immune to electrical interference, making them foolproof in electrical storms. And with the arrival of the computer, fiber optics allow multiple devices to connect all at once, thus providing speedy internet service. Televisions also receive clearer signals and suffer fewer signal losses today than ever before due to Kao's innovation. These advances earned Kao the Nobel Prize in 2009.

FIBER OPTICS, STRANDS THE SIZE OF A HUMAN HAIR—
TYPICALLY .005 INCHES (.0127 CM IN DIAMETER—MADE
OF GLASS OR A FLEXIBLE SILICA MATERIAL, HAVE
TRANSFORMED THE INFORMATION AGE, ALLOWING MORE
DATA TO BE TRANSFERRED MORE EFFICIENTLY THAN
EVER BEFORE.

ENCASED IN A PROTECTIVE SHEATH, A
BUNDLE OF MANY THOUSANDS OF FIBERS
CAN TRANSMIT LIGHT SIGNALS OVER
LONG DISTANCES BECAUSE THE LIGHT IS
CONSTANTLY REFLECTING ALONG THE
INSIDE OF THE GLASS FIBER.

Saint Benedict of Nursia, surprising founder of the first corporation. From a fresco by Fra Angelico.

Corporation

Through the success of partnerships, educated risk-taking, and invested shareholders, corporations have helped shape the way we live.

The phrase "United we stand, divided we fall" is usually associated with patriotism, but it also sums up the premise of incorporation rather succinctly. The concept—coming together to create an organization in which the whole is stronger than the sum of its parts—dates back to the Benedictine Order of the Catholic Church, founded and incorporated in 529 C.E.

The corporation has helped drive business throughout the world by bringing product development, manufacturing, and distribution all under one roof. The ability to diversify tasks yet keep them all "in-house" led to economies of greater scale, lower prices for the consumer, and greater gain for the corporation. This way of doing business, governed by a legal process that recognizes a corporation as a single entity still able to offer protection to its "owners" (or shareholders), greatly spurred innovation. Scientists and engineers working within corporations had funds available for research and development, allowing creativity to flourish.

Today's vast and varied consumer marketplace is, in great part, owed to the development of the corporation.

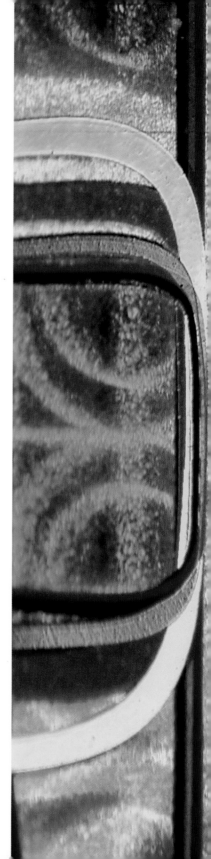

Holography

Sometimes, an invention can just seem like a neat idea—a mere blip on the timeline of tinkering's many achievements. Then, as scientists and innovators begin to find more and more applications, a breakthrough's true power comes to light. Holography is a prime example of this phenomenon.

Holography is a photographic technique that records the light scattered from an object and then presents that light in a way that appears three-dimensional. Dennis Gabor, the Hungarian physicist behind holography, created the first hologram in 1947 using mercury vapor lamps, but he found this experiment to be enormously expensive. Nonetheless, Gabor's discovery attracted widespread attention. When lasers finally appeared in the 1960s, the new technology was able to amplify the intensity of light waves, making holograms economically feasible. The first 3-D images showed a toy train and a bird, and many objects followed, including the first human in 1967. While igniting the interest of many scientists and even earning Gabor a Nobel Prize in Physics in 1971, the practical use of such an invention was yet to be seen.

Even still, the idea of a 3-D image sparked curiosity in many fields. In 1968, Dr. Stephen Benton developed an embossing technique that made mass production of holograms possible—and finally gave them an application. Holograms are very difficult to duplicate (much harder than photographs), so small, embossed holographic images became useful in the fight against counterfeiting. There's no doubt that including holograms on currency, credit cards, and passports has strengthened personal, corporate, and governmental security worldwide.

Artists also began incorporating holography into their work, and today in museums you can even see holograms of deceased celebrities. Engineers and scientists can now compare the before-and-after dimensions of an object, thanks to 3-D imagery, and some doctors use holograms as a teaching tool for medical students. The list spans all types of categories, from mundane to essential, and new uses continue to develop regularly.

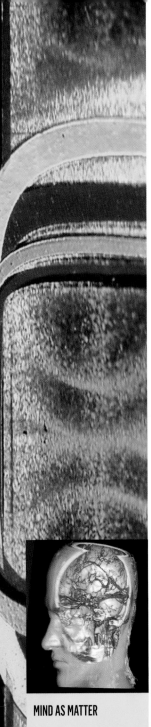

MIND AS MATTER

Holograms comprised of ultrasound images and MRI and CT scans can give doctors a more complete picture of parts of the human body.

Alphabet

It may be difficult to remember how to spell "maneuver," but would you rather draw it?

That was the basic idea behind written communication, or Egyptian hieroglyphics, 5,000 years ago. Historians estimate that during the second millennium B.C.E. a trailblazing tribe of Semitic-speaking people began tweaking the pictographic symbols of their Egyptian neighbors to represent sounds instead of the meanings behind their spoken language. Their work, the Proto-Sinaitic script, is often credited as the first alphabet in which symbols depict the sounds of 22 consonants. Vowels were conspicuously absent, but it was a start.

Centuries later, about the eighth century B.C.E, this system reached the shores of an emerging Greek society. The Greeks modified symbols, added vowels, and placed additional letters at the end of the alphabet. The letters pi, rho, sigma, tau, upsilon, phi, chi, psi, and omega were born, and the Greeks began writing in the *boustrophedon* style, literally meaning "in the same way oxen plow a field," in which the direction of reading and writing alternates from line to line. This style of writing continued for 300 years until it was replaced by the less dizzying left-to-right approach many languages use today.

Pencil and Pen

The death of the pen and pencil has been imminent since the invention of the typewriter, desktop and laptop computers, tablets, smartphones, and any personal device that allows one to type or use a stylus. Yet these stalwart inventions stubbornly live on, seemingly unmatched in their ingenuity and practicality.

These modern tools allow their users to leave behind a trail of symbols, helping readers, mathematicians, and artists create the most important ideas and records in history. A pencil leaves behind a solid residue, a mixture of graphite and clay. Because it is soft and brittle, the mixture is nestled in a protective wooden exterior. Pencil markings are easily rubbed out, and so erasers made of rubber or vinyl have long appeared on the pencil's end, giving grateful writers the ability to correct any errors or omissions.

Pencils have been used in one form or another for hundreds of years. In 1564, residents of Borrowdale, England, discovered a large graphite deposit underground. Shepherds used the graphite to mark and identify their sheep; later, it was used for writing. On its own, the material was delicate, and so the wooden holder was introduced to keep it from crumbling. When a large and superior mine of graphite was discovered in China in 1847, the manufacturers chose a yellow coating for the pencils to honor the emperor. Other pencil manufacturers followed suit and the yellow #2 pencil became a staple in schools and offices around the world. As for the crucial eraser, it was added in 1858 by American Hymen Lipman.

A more permanent partner to the pencil is the ballpoint pen, which leaves a liquid trail behind the tip of the tool rather than a graphite mark. Ballpoint pens have a tiny ball made of brass, steel, or tungsten carbide that rotates in a socket at the tip of the pen. A reservoir holds ink, and a capillary tube carries ink to the ball, which marks across a piece of paper.

Until the early twentieth century, writers who used ink instead of graphite were stuck with quill feathers or fountain pens. In 1938, Hungarian journalist László Bíró grew frustrated by the mess from his leaky fountain pen. Noticing that newspaper ink dried much faster than the ink used in his pen, he placed the thicker liquid into the fountain pen. But this thick ink wouldn't flow, so Bíró and his chemist brother devised a pen tipped with a metal ball bearing that was placed in a socket to keep the ink from spilling over the page. The ballpoint pen revolutionized the way writers touched ink to paper, creating a more convenient tool, whether sitting at a desk or on the go. Libby Sellers of the Design Museum in London remarks that "no longer did you need to worry about ink spills or refills. To be mobile and reliable are two amazing things to be able to accommodate into such a small and humble object."

Aside from a few minor tweaks, the ballpoint pen of today, with its mobile and reliable source of ink, is similar to Bíró's creation. The pencil is also essentially the same as it was 100 years ago, with only minor changes to the content of lead and the design. These objects work so well that they are often overshadowed by other, grander inventions, but most people can find a pen or a pencil in their home or their bag or backpack with little effort. Computers and digital technology have diluted some of the significance of the pen and pencil, but these new gadgets will never entirely replace these small and mighty tools.

Today, it may be impossible to separate cameras from the photographs that they create, but the earliest models didn't produce a physical image at all. Instead, an aperture fitted with an adjustable lens projected an image from outside onto a surface in a darkened room. At first, there was no way of capturing the picture other than tracing it by hand. Over time, inventors created smaller camera obscuras—these portable versions were simple wooden boxes with a lens on one side and a piece of frosted glass across from it that displayed the image.

Shown above is one of the first daguerreotype cameras available for sale to the public, accompanied by the earliest known portrait photograph still in existence. The self-portrait is by Robert Cornelius, an American photographer.

Camera

In 1839, Louis Daguerre presented his method of using light and chemistry to create a permanent image, called a *daguerreotype*, from a camera obscura before the French Academy of Sciences. The process revolutionized the world.

The equipment consisted of five main components: the camera box; silver-plated sheets of copper (which over time were replaced with film); a light-control system using an adjustable aperture and shutter; the lens that directed light onto the copper sheets; and the optical system, which the user looked through to focus the picture.

Modern single-lens reflex (SLR) cameras using film were designed on the same premise. The internal working parts of our portable, handheld cameras include an optical lens, mirror, translucent focusing screen (made of ground glass), prism, eyepiece, and film. When you look through the eyepiece, you see an image that's traveled through the lens and bounced off the mirror onto the glass focusing screen. The prism

above the focusing screen then flips the image at a right angle without reversing it and reflects it onto the eyepiece. Without the prism, you would see the image upside down—as it appears on the focusing screen. (This process is actually very similar to that of a submarine's periscope!)

When the photographer snaps a picture, the interior mirror moves up, causing the viewfinder to go black, blocking excess light from entering through the eyepiece, and directing the light and the image to shine up onto the light-sensitive film. Next, the shutter closes and the mirror moves back down into place. The shutter speed, which is set by the photographer, controls how long the shutter is open, the duration of time that the mirror remains in the up position, and how much light is let into the camera.

For a digital single-lens

reflex camera (DSLR), the concept is basically the same, except that the image is captured as a digital file with electronic sensors instead of being recorded on film.

Throughout the decades since Daguerre's presentation, photography has recorded our histories (both personal and global), introduced us to others in foreign places, and informed us of events that shape our world. Today, small yet powerful cameras in smartphones ensure that a photo is always just a click away, no matter where you go. This medium inspires, entertains, and provokes, and as it continues to evolve through a digital age and beyond, its power to influence remains boundless.

I have not failed. I've just found 10,000 ways that won't work.

— THOMAS A. EDISON

IRONICALLY, EDISON HAD LOST MOST OF HIS HEARING AS A BOY BUT SUCCEEDED IN DEVELOPING THE FIRST MACHINE TO CAPTURE SOUND AND PLAY IT BACK.

100 INVENTIONS

Phonograph

Thomas Edison considered the phonograph, the first device to record sound, his favorite among all his inventions. A long cylinder amplified the sound from Edison's voice, and the sound waves hit a thin membrane inside the cylinder called a diaphragm. The diaphragm was connected to a sharp needle, which shook from the vibrations of his voice. The needle left indentations along a piece of tinfoil wrapped inside the cylinder. As Edison spoke, he rotated a crank that turned the cylinder while the needle gouged a pattern along the surface of the tinfoil. To play back the sound, Edison placed the same needle at the starting position, using less pressure. As the needle ran along the groove it had created, it produced scratching sounds that mimicked Edison's voice. An amplifier made the sound loud enough for listening ears. None of these early recordings remain, since after only a few plays the tinfoil was destroyed, but it is widely acknowledged that the first words ever recorded by Edison were "Mary had a little lamb."

Edison had many plans for the phonograph, including use as a dictation machine, an aid for the blind, a music box, and a recording device for the telephone. But some uses emerged that Edison never imagined. During World War I, a special phonograph was created for the US Army to raise the spirits of soldiers. The phonograph brought music to many people who otherwise could not have heard it (and who would gladly pay for the chance to), and the recording industry was born.

Later designs used a sturdier flat disc instead of a cylinder and played back on a device called the gramophone. Larger records allowed recordings to play for longer periods of time. In 1948, Columbia Records created the long-playing (LP) record, a descendant of Edison's early inventions, which later launched musicians like Elvis Presley and the Beatles into the mainstream. LPs also allow us to hear the voices of other influential figures of that time, including Edison himself. Devices such as cassettes, CDs, and digital files have almost replaced all traces of the phonograph, but it remains an important predecessor.

Graphical User Interface

Sometimes something *isn't* more than just a pretty face. That's the case with the graphical user interface, a fancy way of describing the images, icons, and text on a computer screen. Often called GUI (pronounced "gooey"), the program puts a pretty face on computer operating systems and brings structure to the user experience. Microsoft's Windows and Apple's Macintosh are two of the most popular examples of GUI programs.

GUI typically includes a pointing device (or cursor), icons, a desktop screen, windows, and menus with dropdown functions. Beyond the graphic icons, an important goal of GUI is to make it easier for users to move data from one application to another—for example, to copy an image created in one program into a different document. Prior to well-designed GUI programs, computer users had to be fluent in the text commands required to operate the computer via keyboard. Before that, punch cards (index cards with punched holes) would be inserted into the computer to facilitate each and every command.

Today, advancements in GUI have made computer literacy accessible to everyone. Thanks to point-and-click technology, the world is at our fingertips—and we don't have to understand much more than how to move a mouse in order to operate the system. Today, even toddlers can figure out how to get around on a touch-screen or work a mouse.

Although an obvious example of GUI can be seen in the personal computer, many electronic devices now use graphical user interfaces as well: the touch-screen directory at the mall, smartphones, ATMs, point-of-purchase registers, and more. The first GUIs were introduced in the 1970s by the Xerox Corporation, but it wasn't until a decade later that Apple made them cool—and ubiquitous. By the 1980s, previous deterrents, such as lack of central processing unit (CPU) power and low-quality monitors, were becoming less of an issue as technological advancements put increasingly sophisticated computers within financial reach of consumers. The innovation also vaulted productivity to new heights as work became increasingly computer-centric.

In the future, GUI advancements will continue to define the best in computer technology, providing distinction between operating systems. It will also likely creep into other realms of our lives, as innovators find new ways to incorporate touchscreens into our homes, cars, and personal devices.

Videotape

Before compact discs, Blu-ray, Apple TV, DVRs, and pay-per-view, home movie nights involved an extra step. Visiting the local video store was a weekly activity for many families: children and adults roamed the aisles picking movies to rent or buy to watch at home over the weekend.

It may be difficult to find a video store in town these days, but the development of videotape and the industries it spawned changed the way people viewed their entertainment, upturning conventions that had been in place since the beginning of TV and film.

The dawn of the television age brought about several advances in how programming was brought to the masses. Film stock used in motion pictures was expensive and easily degraded, and developing the film took time. "Live"

television, the only other option, was limited by human error and the need for all the players in a program to be together at one time.

The evolution of videotape—the recording of sounds and images onto magnetic tape that could then be replayed—began in the early 1950s. Television giants such as RCA and entertainer Bing Crosby's production company worked on adapting technology used in the music recording business, with some early success, but the images produced were grainy and hard to make out. The technology at that time required miles of tape on which to store data, making it expensive and impractical. Despite these drawbacks, a videotaped performance of singer Dorothy Collins was included during the live broadcast of *The Jonathan*

Winters Show in 1956, and the era of videotape was born.

The first commercially viable system was developed by an American company, Ampex, in 1956. Its "quad" system used 2-inch (5-cm) tape that four magnetic heads ran across, recording images and sound and allowing the entire width of the tape to be used, minimizing the amount of material needed to store data. In the mid-1960s, Sony developed a videotape recorder for home use, and the industry exploded.

Videotape would remain popular for public use until digital recording on compact discs or hard drives became widely available to consumers in the twenty-first century. However, video-tape is still used for film and television production today due to its inexpensive cost and its lengthy lifespan.

According to Avram Pitch, online editorial director for *Laptop* magazine, **"13 MILLION BLANK VHS AND CASSETTE TAPES WERE SOLD IN 2012," EVEN THOUGH THE TECHNOLOGY IS OBSOLETE.**

Television

It would be hard—no, impossible—
to imagine today's world without
television. At the press of a button,
you can travel the world, go back
in time, watch athletes breaking
records, and even have a view of
wars raging on the other side
of the world from the safety of
your living room.

Television has transformed news, entertainment, and education. But few people are aware of how it actually works. Modern television is really three inventions. First, there's the TV camera, which turns pictures and sound into a signal carried by the second invention, the transmitter. The TV transmitter generates radio waves, invisible patterns of electricity and magnetism that travel through the air at the speed of light, 186,000 miles per second (299,388 km/s). The third invention is the TV receiver, which captures the signal and

turns it back into picture and sound. The TV image on the screen is not really a continuous moving image, but a rapid-fire succession of still images that are fused together by the human brain to make a moving image. The TV camera captures a new still image more than 24 times per second to create the illusion of a moving image.

Light detectors inside the TV camera scan an image line by line, turning it into 525 different lines of colored light that are then transmitted to viewers as a video signal. At the same

time, microphones capture the sound that goes with the picture and transmit it as a separate audio signal. Both are then transferred to a powerful transmitter that sends the signals over the air. If you have cable television, signals are piped into your home along a fiber optic cable. If you have satellite television, the signals are bounced up to a satellite and back again to your home. However the signal gets to a TV set, the receiver in your television treats it exactly the same, doing in reverse

what the TV camera does to turn the signals into the images and sounds.

Modern liquid-crystal display (LCD) TVs have millions of tiny picture elements called pixels. Each pixel is made up of three smaller red, green, and blue sub-pixels that are turned on or off by the signal. A plasma screen is similar to an LCD screen except that each pixel is a kind of miniature lamp glowing with plasma, a very hot form of gas.

Television has come a long way from its invention in the 1930s. On September 7, 1922, inventor Philo T. Farnsworth painted a square of glass black and scratched a straight line down its center. He then separated an image into a series of lines of electricity and sent radio waves to a receiver, which picked up the image and displayed it. Farnsworth's invention was challenged by Russian-American engineer Vladimir Zworykin, who had developed a similar device. In 1934, the US Patent Office awarded the patent to Farnsworth.

Farnsworth knew he had invented something important, but he wasn't sure he had done a good thing. According to his son Kent, Farnsworth "felt that he had created kind of a monster, a way for people to waste a lot of their lives."

Electric Guitar

As music increased in popularity in the nineteenth century, the size of concert halls also increased to accommodate the masses. The larger spaces demanded more volume and the needs of musicians began to change. The Smithsonian credits the rise of big band music, phonographic recordings, and radio with the desire for a louder guitar. At first, artists tried megaphones and steel strings to amplify the sound of the acoustic guitar.

The first big breakthrough came in 1931, when George Beauchamp developed a device in which a current, passing through a coil of wire wrapped around a magnet, succeeded in amplifying a string's vibrations. Beauchamp and his partner, Adolph Rickenbacker, created a lap steel electric guitar called the Frying Pan. The guitar would rest on a player's lap as he moved a metal slide along the steel strings. The musician plucked the strings with his other hand, manipulating the pitch.

The Frying Pan, however, was not an overnight success. At first shunned by traditionalists, the electric guitar faced

Rock and roll music's impact on culture during the last half of the twentieth century was undeniable, and no instrument was more pivotal to the music genre's success than the electric guitar. The instrument works by converting vibrations into electrical sound signals. The vibrations, or notes, are sent to an amplifier, allowing more people to hear the melody across greater distances.

criticism that the sound was not authentic. The mixed reviews coincided with the Great Depression, when few could even afford the new instruments. Eventually, however, country and jazz musicians jumped to the electric guitar's defense, praising the louder sound, which was now able to compete with other instruments in an ensemble.

In 1947, designer Paul Bigsby and country singer Merle Travis teamed up on an updated design for an electric guitar, one more similar to today's version. In the 1950s, Leo Fender had the first major commercial success, and the Fender guitar influenced a new wave of guitar manufacturing, popularizing the novel design. The Gibson guitar emerged as Fender's biggest competitor in 1952, and as rock and roll took off, teenagers and aspiring musicians used the technology to usher in a new era of music, making the electric guitar synonymous with rock and roll.

Beyond the bedrooms of sixteen-year-old strummers and expanded concert halls, the electric guitar also made large-scale, open-air performances possible, paving the way for a little gathering called Woodstock. Some of our greatest rock stars—Elvis Presley, the Beatles, the Rolling Stones, Joan Jett, and Jimi Hendrix, just to name a few—might never have earned their fame without the electric guitar. For that achievement, this invention deserves a round of applause.

Printing Press

The movable-type printing press was the invention of Johannes Gutenberg, a German goldsmith who perfected the invention between 1440 and 1450. To use the press, an operator put metal letters in a tray, applied ink to them, and placed the tray over paper or parchment. A large screw mechanism would then press the tray with great force into the paper, producing a printed sheet. When something else needed printing, the operator simply arranged a new metal letters in the tray.

Gutenberg Bible (top) and miniature press model (bottom).

That doesn't sound revolutionary until you consider that at the time, books were not printed but copied by hand. As a result, very few books were produced, and each was worth its weight in gold.

In Europe during the Middle Ages, just about the only people who could read and write were monks and other churchmen. Gutenberg's movable-type press, however, came at a time when Europe was ready and able to spread literacy. He rapidly developed his printing system. In 1450 he printed his first book, a Latin Bible. In 1452, he printed and sold 200 copies of what is now known as the Gutenberg Bible. In spite of Gutenberg's efforts to keep his invention a secret, printing presses multiplied rapidly. Before 1500, some 2,500 presses could be found in Europe. The immediate effect of all these presses was to multiply the output and cut the cost of books.

Gutenberg's printing press was the beginning of an "information revolution" similar to the growth of the internet today. With more and more reading materials available, literacy spread across the continent. The availability of books and documents increased the sharing of information, ideas, and literature, giving birth to the modern world.

It is a press, certainly, but a press from which shall flow in inexhaustible streams...Through it, God will spread His Word. A spring of truth shall flow from it: like a new star it shall scatter the darkness of ignorance and cause a light heretofore unknown to shine amongst men.

—JOHANNES GUTENBERG

Virtual Reality

Wondering what life would be like on the Moon—all while we remain tethered to Earth—used to be the job of children and daydreamers. But the advancement of computer displays and 3D technology allows us to immerse ourselves in worlds as various as car racing and battle.

The definition of virtual reality as we understand it today was commercialized by computer scientist Jaron Lanier in the 1980s. Lanier's fantastic vision included interactive, computer-generated environments that allowed users to travel through space and time to visit other lands or wander through the human body. But a filmmaker named Morton Heilig in the 1950s is probably responsible for the first commercial virtual-reality experience. Using his "Sensorama" console, viewers watching a film while sitting in a chair that

could move were able to smell odors and feel sensations associated with what was on the screen. In the mid-1960s, computer scientist Ivan Sutherland, funded by NASA, developed systems linked to computers that supplied graphics and sound and that later developed into early flight simulators. Other industries, including architecture, construction, and the medical field, also embraced the emerging technology.

Virtual reality systems for consumer use developed in the 1990s. Wearing headsets and goggles, participants would stand in a three-sided booth that displayed images of an alternative environment. Gloves with applied computer sensors allowed the individual to open doors, travel pathways, and change perspective, all while feeling immersed in this "virtual" world. Critics of this early technology argued that the immersive experience was not rich enough, as it did not allow participants to forget about their actual surroundings.

Video game programmers nudged the concept further, creating graphics and interactive features that employ a sensor to enable the user's body to deliver directive cues in a game. The sensor hardware includes a video camera for face recognition and body detection, a depth-detection component, and an array of four microphones to pick up sounds made by the different players in the room. The most exciting development in virtual reality in years, however, is the Oculus Rift, announced in 2014, whose headset provides more range of movement, a wider field of vision, and less lag time.

Virtual worlds take time and money to create. But programming that allows users to smell the enticing odors of a Thai food stall in Bangkok or feel the heat of the desert winds in California may, at last, be closer than we think.

TRAINING FOR SPACE

NASA astronauts use virtual reality hardware inside the Space Vehicle Mockup Facility in order to practice tasks they will undertake when deployed to the International Space Station.

Telegraph

American inventor Samuel Morse perfected the electric telegraph, a device that delivers a series of electric impulses along  insulated wires. He sent his first telegraph message in 1844 from Washington, DC, to Baltimore.

Morse's electric telegraph had three parts, all hooked together by a wire: a battery to supply the electricity; a key used to complete or break the electrical circuit, and an electromagnet, consisting of a coil of insulated wire turned around an iron core. In early electric telegraphs, the battery consisted of a glass jar filled with a chemical solution (usually copper sulfate) with copper and zinc electrodes immersed in the solution. The chemical reaction between the electrodes and the solution produced electrical voltage. The key in early telegraphs originally consisted of two pieces of copper or bronze that could be pressed together to complete the circuit. The telegraph's electromagnet pulled on a piece of iron when an electric current passed through the coiled wire.

Messages traveled along the wire from one telegraph to the receiver on another telegraph when the operator pressed down on the key, completing the circuit and creating marks on a paper tape used to record the message—dots for short periods of electrical connection, dashes for longer connections. Each letter in the alphabet had its own pattern of dots and dashes (which would come to be known as Morse code) so that the messages could be translated into language.

The public quickly accepted Morse's telegraph, and the invention revolutionized distance communication. Morse code messages traveled with the speed of electricity, linking cities and towns with instant communication for the first time in history.

In 1858, a telegraph line was laid across the Atlantic Ocean from the United States to Europe. By 1861, Western Union had installed the first transcontinental telegraph line across the United States. It wasn't until the twentieth century that new technologies overshadowed this extraordinary invention.

The telegraph, invented in the late 1830s, revolutionized long-distance communication. It thus became the ancestor of the telephone, fax machine, radio, television, and even the internet.

Morse Code

Disguised in a language of dots and dashes, Morse code helps people communicate instantly over a telegraph.

A	.-	F	..-.	K	-.-	Q	--.-	V	...-
B	-...	G	--.	L	.-..	R	.-.	W	.--
C	-.-.	H	....	M	--	S	...	X	-..-
D	-..	I	..	N	-.	T	-	Y	-.--
E	.	J	.---	O	---	U	..-	Z	--..
		P	.--.						

Paul Saffo, a fellow for the Institute of the Future, explains to the *New York Times* how Morse code will be kept alive:

"MORSE WILL NOW BECOME THE OBJECT OF LOVING PASSION BY RADIOHEADS, MUCH AS ANOTHER 'DEAD' LANGUAGE, LATIN, IS KEPT ALIVE TODAY BY LATIN-SPEAKING ENTHUSIASTS AROUND THE WORLD."

There are too many instances to count of Morse code relaying vital information. For instance, the only surviving accounts of the sinking of the *Titanic* in 1912 are the Morse code transcripts sent out by the doomed crew. In 1966, Admiral Jeremiah Denton, a POW in Hanoi, was able to blink in Morse code during a television interview to alert American authorities that the North Vietnamese were torturing American captives. In 1973, during a war games exercise, the Navy destroyer USS *Wood* lost power and became stranded. Without any other means of communication, the ship's crew used battery-powered lanterns to flash Morse code and alert a nearby Russian destroyer of the *Wood*'s position.

When communicating by Morse code (named after its inventor, Samuel Morse), the sender and receiver follow an international standard in order to decipher a message. The short signals are called "dits" (represented by dots), and long signals are calls "dahs" (represented by dashes). Dits and dahs are used in a pattern that represents a specific letter. For example, the most well-known usage of Morse code, SOS, is three dits (S), followed by three dahs (O), and then three more dits (S). The code requires users to allow a standard amount of time to elapse between each letter, so the message comes across clearly and accurately.

Today, Morse code is no longer used by any major organization, as other technology has replaced the once-critical method of communication. The Federal Communication Commission dropped the Morse code requirement for ham radio operators in 2006, and even the Coast Guard has stopped listening for SOS signals at sea. However, some enthusiasts hope to keep the system relevant.

Although no standard uses may exist, Morse code still has the potential to emerge as effective communication in unanticipated ways. Almost anything can send a message in Morse code—a telegraph, a flashlight, finger taps, or blinks.

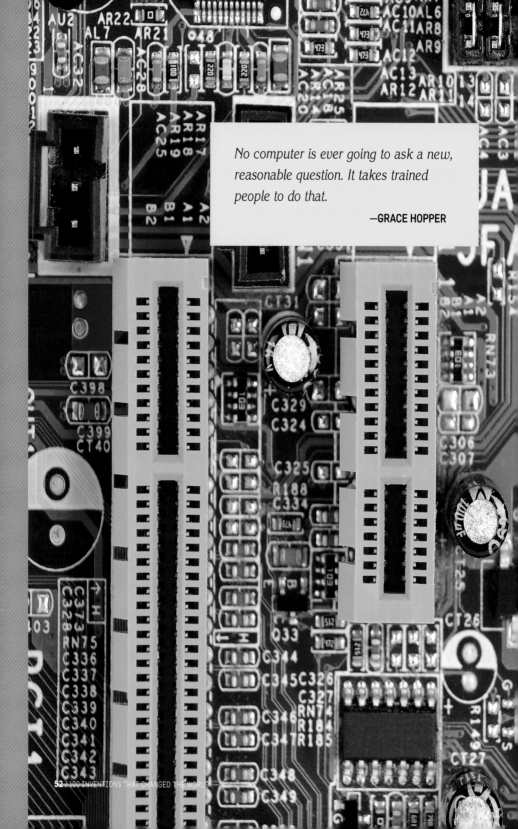

> No computer is ever going to ask a new, reasonable question. It takes trained people to do that.
>
> —GRACE HOPPER

Computer

The first modern computers were cumbersome machines designed to solve complicated mathematical questions. Today's computers do much more than math, but the language they speak is still one of calculation, storing each piece of information as a number.

English inventor, scientist, and mathematician Charles Babbage is credited with conceiving of the first computer, which he called the "Difference Engine," in the early 1830s. It was designed to solve mathematical computations. In 1991, the Science Museum in London built Babbage's computer and discovered that the visionary inventor's machine worked.

Replacing a bad vacuum tube meant checking among ENIAC's 19,000 tubes.

ENIAC (Electronic Numerical Integrator and Computer) was one of the first digital computers. Built in 1954, it weighed 30 tons (27,215.5 kg) and was powered by thousands of vacuum tubes, capacitors, relays, and electrical equipment. ENIAC lacked an operating system, but its legacy can be found in the personal computers of today.

Although in 1943 IBM president Tom Watson famously said, "I think there is a world market for maybe five computers," advances in electronics (transistors), the application of semiconductors, and the integrated circuit enabled reductions in size and increases in power that paved the way for a much more robust prognosis.

Today, a computer is a programmable machine that responds to a specific set of defined instructions. It consists of hardware (the machinery and housing for its electronics) and software (the programs that contain the data used by the computer). The hardware includes a central processing unit (CPU) that controls an operating system, which directs your inputs (keyboard, mouse, or microphone), outputs (LCD display or printer), memory, and storage. Computers are now everywhere, and there's more to come: Computers that learn on their own, brain–computer interfacing, and quantum computers that utilize fiber optic technology are all on the horizon.

Video Games

On Christmas Day in 2014, joy in millions of households across the world was replaced by disappointment. A group called the Lizard Squad hacked into Microsoft's Xbox Live and Sony's PlayStation, both video-game platforms, making it impossible to connect to the internet and run the systems for more than 150 million users.

Service was eventually restored, but the hacking soured Christmas for many kids (and adults) eager to play new games. Video games have become so common—and so sophisticated and realistic—that it's easy to forget that only 40 years ago they featured simple black-and-white blips simulating balls bouncing on a TV screen.

Today video games are played with controllers that connect to specialized computers called consoles. Consoles have a central processing unit (CPU), a user control interface that allows the gamer to take charge of the action, a software kernel that provides the interface between the various pieces of hardware in the system, and video and audio outlets. Video game designers and programmers code each individual game with a series of algorithms that drive outcomes based on players' choices throughout the game.

Current systems also offer solid-state memory cards for storing saved games and personal information. Systems like PlayStation have DVD drives that allow gamers to upload different games, and all game consoles provide a video system that is compatible with television sets. The software for today's computer gaming systems has evolved to include realistic, full-color graphics, multilayered sound effects, and pathways for very complex interactions between gamers and the system. It also allows gamers to interact with other players all over the world through the internet interface. But maybe most importantly, a huge variety of games is available. Some popular games include Grand Theft Auto V, Call of Duty: Ghosts, inFAMOUS Second Son, Titan Fall, and Minecraft.

Ralph Baer, who died at age 92 in 2014 after a long career in the radio and television industry, is credited with inventing the first video game console. One day in 1966, he was sitting on a curb outside a Manhattan bus station waiting for a friend when he realized how he might make his idea for playing games on TV work.

"It was basically a demonstration of how to put a spot on a screen, how to move it laterally, horizontally, and vertically, and how to color it, how to color the background," he told a *Washington Post* reporter. After much work, Baer came up with a console that attached to a TV set and played an electronic ping-pong game later called Pong—the ancestor of today's realistic and elaborate video games. Video games are now a $10.5 billion industry.

SPREADING IDEAS / **55**

Satellite

Satellites circle our planet in regular orbits. When objects such as meteors draw close to Earth, they become trapped by the planet's gravity and burn up in the atmosphere. Satellites, however, are launched at precisely calculated speeds—fast enough to maintain a balance between a satellite's velocity and Earth's gravitational pull.

If a satellite is traveling at the predicted speed, it will repeatedly "fall" toward Earth, but Earth's curvature and the satellite's speed result in it falling in orbit around the planet—instead of crashing down. The exact speed needed to keep a satellite in orbit depends on the height of the orbit—the higher it travels, the less speed required for the

satellite to overcome gravity and avoid burning up.

There are several accepted zones of satellite orbits around Earth. One is called low Earth orbit (LEO), extend from 100 to 1,250 miles (161–2,011 km) above Earth's surface. This is the zone where the ISS orbits and where the US space shuttle orbited previously.

satellite appears to be fixed in the sky.

This allows the satellite to keep a stable connection with stationary ground antennas. Fixed satellites can receive and send hundreds of billions of voice, data, and video transmissions.

Regardless of its purpose, every operating satellite has three main parts: a power system, usually nuclear or solar; an antenna to transmit data and to receive radio wave instructions from Earth; and a payload, such as a camera or particle detector, to collect information.

Satellites were the stuff of science fiction as recently as 58 years ago, when the Soviet Union launched the first real operating Earth satellite, Sputnik I, on October 4, 1957. Sputnik's success triggered the "space race" between the United States and the USSR. The United States launched its first artificial satellite, Explorer 1, on January 31, 1958. Today, besides Russia and the United States, more than 40 other countries have launched their own satellites. A sky so full of satellites faces a new problem—space junk. So many dead satellites, spent rockets, and pieces of space hardware now circle the planet that they pose a hazard to operating satellites. More than 21,000 pieces of space trash larger than 4 inches (10 cm), plus half a million bits between ¼ and 4 inches (0.64–10 cm), are now estimated to orbit around Earth. Even tiny pieces of junk, when moving at high speed, can destroy an operating satellite.

Most satellites also work in LEO. Most communications satellites occupy a different zone, however, designed to keep them in geostationary orbit. This is a zone above Earth's equator at an altitude of 22,236 miles (35,785 km). In this zone, the rate of "fall" around Earth is the same as the speed of Earth's rotation. Thus, from the ground, the

Explorer 1, America's first Earth satellite, in 1958.

))) Telephone (((

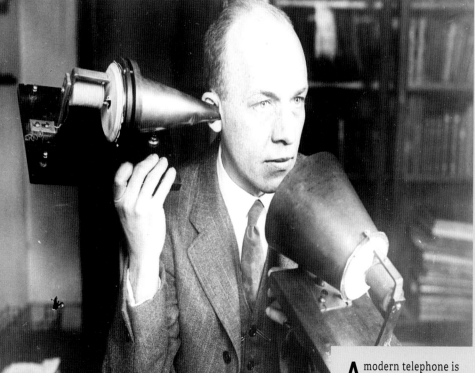

BELL'S FIRST TELEPHONE
This photo from *The Detroit News* shows Bell's first telephone.

It's so common that everyone has one but hardly notices it—until it rings. You may take it for granted, but the humble telephone stands proudly among the greatest inventions of all time. Before the telephone was invented, it would take weeks or even months for written messages to reach those for whom they were intended.

A modern telephone is a complete system. Whether it is a landline phone or a cell phone, a typical phone handset has a loudspeaker at the top that presses against your ear and a microphone at the bottom near your mouth. In traditional landline phones, when you speak into the mouthpiece, the sound energy in your voice makes a plastic disk called a diaphragm vibrate, moving a coil nearer to or farther from a magnet. This movement generates an electric current in the coil that corresponds to the sound of your voice: If you talk loudly, a large current is generated; if you talk softly, the current is smaller. The microphone turns the sound of your voice into electrical energy. The loudspeaker in a telephone works in the opposite way: It takes an incoming electrical current and converts the electrical energy back into sound energy. In some phones, the loudspeaker and the microphone units are identical, just wired up in opposite ways.

A cell phone, unlike a landline phone, has no external wires. Instead, it uses radio waves to output a signal. Landline phones and cell phones have the same structure, except that landline phones rely on telephone lines, whereas cell phones use advanced electronics to send out radio waves in all directions until they hit a cell tower. The cell tower then sends out radio waves to the person you want to call.

In the 1870s, two inventors, Alexander Graham Bell and Elisha Gray, both independently designed devices that could transmit speech electrically. Both men rushed their designs to the patent office, but Bell arrived there first and patent his invention, which he dubbed the "telephone."

Bell's success resulted from his attempts to improve the telegraph, which had been developed in the 1830s and 1840s by Samuel Morse and others. The great drawback of the telegraph was that only one message could be sent at a time. Bell's extensive knowledge of the nature of sound waves enabled him to conceive of a way to use electricity to have two messages or conversations at the same time.

In June 1875, Bell was experimenting with a technique he called the "harmonic telegraph" when he discovered he could hear sound over a wire. He developed this technique and on March 10, 1876, he spoke through a new device to his assistant, Thomas A. Watson, in the next room, saying, "Mr. Watson. Come here. I want to see you"—the world's first telephone message.

Abacus

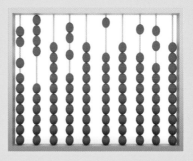

Before computers and calculators, the abacus was the most significant mathematical tool used for thousands of years.

Derived from the Latin word *abax*, meaning "tablet," the abacus evolved in a time before pen and paper, and first models were "counting boards" that served as aids for remembering large numbers. Merchants no longer had to rely on their fingers, allowing more accurate counts. Abaci later developed into the precursor to the calculator. The oldest surviving abacus is the Salamis tablet, which dates back to 300 B.C.E. This early model, made of marble, used pebbles placed in various groups on the tablet's markings to make calculations. Different cultures developed their own designs over the years, finally resulting in the familiar wood frame with sliding beads that we know today.

The concept is simple for those with basic mathematical skills. Beads slide vertically along the wires. The rods farthest to the right represent numbers in the ones position, with each successive rod to the left representing tens, hundreds, thousands, and so forth. More complicated systems involve placeholders to keep track of the larger numbers.

Paper

Paper is more than just a writing surface, and today it would be hard to imagine life without it.

While the process of papermaking has remained essentially the same over hundreds of years, early papermakers from China and Europe would have difficulty recognizing the equipment in modern paper factories. In today's paper mills, timber is soaked in water and the bark is removed. A chipper cuts the pieces to a small size, and the chips are carried to the digester, where the wood fibers are separated further. The next step is to bleach the pulp and rinse it with water. As the pulp travels down the "wire," a moving belt of wire or mesh, the water drains away and the fibers stick to each other, forming a paper web. After the paper is dried and coated with different pigments and glossing substances, it is cut to appropriate sizes and packaged to be sent away for many uses.

Papermaking was invented in China sometime before 105 C.E., when Emperor Ts'ai Lun recorded its existence. Early Chinese paper was made from hemp waste that was washed, soaked, and beaten to a pulp using a wooden mallet. In Japan and Korea,
paper spread along with Buddhism, and the invention traveled to the Middle East and Europe on the Silk Road. In Europe, the development of the printing press made paper the vehicle for the written word, bringing Martin Luther's Bible to the masses and spreading ideas about science, technology, and history. In his book *The Paper Trail: An Unexpected History of the World's Greatest Invention*, Alexander Monro declares, "History's most galvanizing ideas have hitched a lift on its surface."

Today, more than 400 million tons (362.8 million kg) of paper and cardboard are manufactured and each American consumes 675 pounds (306 kg) of paper every year. We read magazines, books, and newspapers, all printed on paper. Cardboard, a form of heavy-duty paper, is used to ship 95 percent of all manufactured goods, since it is much lighter than traditional wooden crates. Official documents like birth certificates and marriage licenses take shape on paper. Cereal boxes and egg cartons package our groceries. Paper is also used during construction as insulation, wallpaper, and shingles, and in masking tape and sandpaper. From toilet paper to currency, paper will undoubtedly be in demand far into the future.

Radio

No one at the time could even imagine how radio (and later, television) would change the globe. Radio remains relevant today as a conduit for entertainment, news, and information, although most listen to it primarily while driving. But with our reliance on electricity and the internet, radio is often the only way to receive reliable information in the case of a power outage when all other systems of intel gathering are down.

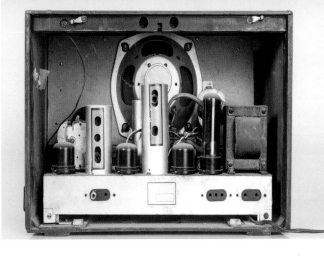

Who invented the radio? That's not a simple question to answer. While the inventors of many other world-changing devices and technologies are easy to pinpoint, that is not the case with the humble radio. This is because no individual can lay sole claim to its invention.

The Scottish scientist James Clerk Maxwell kicked things off in 1867 by predicting the existence of radio waves—electromagnetic radiation with wavelengths longer than infrared light. In 1887, German physicist Heinrich Hertz produced radio waves in a laboratory setting. Hertz discovered that the waves could transfer sound from one point to another.

After Hertz's work, many people tried their hands at developing the electronic components needed to transmit sound and receive it using radio waves. Chief among them was Guglielmo Marconi, an Italian physicist and engineer. Marconi's version of the device could transmit and receive radio waves in wireless communication. By 1895, he was able to transmit radio signals across about 1½ miles (2.4 km). For his invention, Marconi was awarded a British patent.

But he wasn't done. In 1897, Marconi established a radio station on an island off the coast of Great Britain and continued to improve radio transmission. In 1899, he transmitted messages across the English Channel to France. In 1902, he transmitted radio waves all the way across the Atlantic Ocean from England to Canada and the United States. For his contributions to the development of radio, Marconi was awarded the Nobel Prize for Physics in 1909.

The first commercial radio broadcast occurred in New York City on January 13, 1910, when opera singers Enrico Caruso and Emmy Destinn sang arias which, according to the *New York Times*, were "trapped and magnified by the dictograph directly from the stage and borne by wireless Hertzian waves over the turbulent waters of the sea to transcontinental and coastwise ships and over the mountainous peaks and undulating valleys of the country."

Calculus

Author and mathematician
W. S. Anglin notes,

"MATHEMATICS IS NOT A CAREFUL MARCH DOWN A WELL-CLEARED HIGHWAY, BUT A JOURNEY INTO A STRANGE WILDERNESS."

High school math students might believe the devil invented calculus, but they'd be wrong. Two gifted men are credited with creating the mathematical system that predicts the rate of change (differential calculus) and accumulation (integral calculus).

In the 1670s, English physicist and mathematician Sir Isaac Newton and German mathematician and philosopher Gottfried Wilhelm Leibniz were searching independently for a way to unify algebra and geometry, the mathematical theories of their day, in order to more precisely explain the nature of the world. Each scientist wrote a complete system of calculus and accused the other of plagiarism. What ensued was a bitter dispute in which credit was eventually awarded to Newton.

In truth, however, both men were responsible for creating the mathematical system that gave us a universal language to define the world around us. Simply put, without calculus we would not be able to formulate birth rates in the field of biology, compute marginal cost and marginal revenue in economics, or predict maximum profit in a specific economic setting. Calculus allows us to construct mathematical models of how things will change and the effects those changes will have on a system. Subjects as diverse as the study of music, the universe, economics, medicine, and engineering, among others, all require calculus to be explored and understood.

One way to comprehend what calculus is and why anyone would work so hard to create such an abstract, complex system is to look at what Newton was trying to explain. In studying gravity, the physicist found that the speed of a falling object increases with every split second, but there were no mathematical systems available to describe the object at those precise moments in time. Algebra and geometry were practiced in Newton's era, but no one had ever created a relationship between the two disciplines. Newton merged the two systems to create new methods and terminology to quantify the force of a falling object (gravity), the slope of a curve, and motion. In his *Principia: The Mathematical Principles of Natural Philosophy*, published in 1687, Newton presented his theories of "infinitesimal calculus," that is, the mechanics that could explain the movement of the Moon and tides, how Earth turned on an axis, and the shape of a comet's orbit.

Leibniz's brilliant contribution to calculus can be seen in the carefully drawn symbols and rules he used to explain his work. Today we use his form of writing instead of Newton's clumsier style of notation. In fact, most mathematicians believe we have Leibniz to thank for the equal sign.

Arabic Numerals

Despite their names, French fries are not from France and the Arabic numeral system—ten digits from zero to nine in a positional notation decimal system—is not from Arabia.

In fact, it was mathematicians from India who developed the decimal numeral system around 500 CE. The concept, which includes using zero as a placeholder and the indication of the value of numbers through their placement (i.e., having a ones column, a tens column, a hundreds column, etc.), was revolutionary. Prior to this system, the value of 30 would have been denoted with only a 3, and the actual value would have been understood through context. The new system made it possible to distinguish meaning in the absence of context, communicate value through placement, calculate fractions, and recognize zero as a value.

In Europe, Italian mathematician Leonardo Fibonacci popularized Arabic numerals in his book *Liber Abaci* in 1202, and thanks to the invention of the printing press in Europe in the fifteenth century, the use of the numerals and the decimal system became widespread.

But how the numbers 0, 1, 2, 3, 4, 5, 6, 7, 8, and 9 came to look as they do remains a subject of debate. Some scholars believe the symbols evolved from Arabic letters, while others suspect the numbers graphically represented the number of angles contained within the symbol.

What we do know is that the foreign symbols caught on. Although Roman numerals remained in use for clock faces, lists, written outlines, and other traditional writings, the popularity of the positional notation system and Arabic numerals multiplied exponentially, making the Arabic innovation the most widely used numeric system in the world to this day.

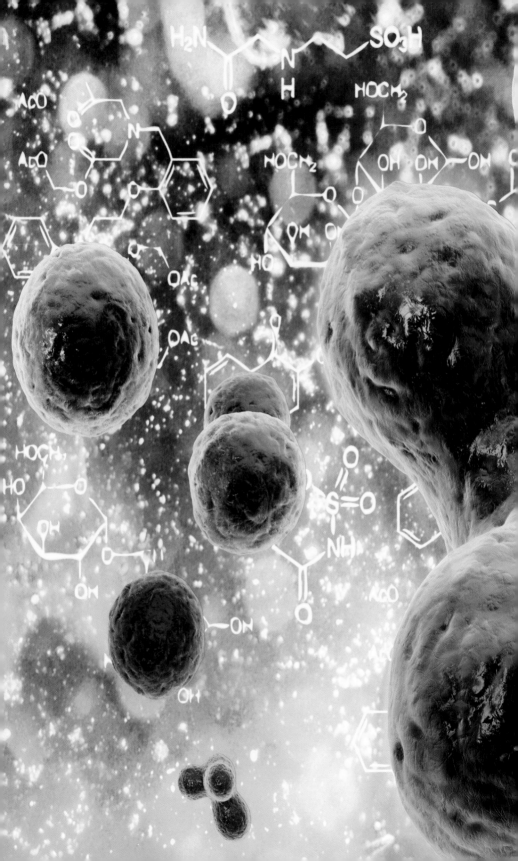

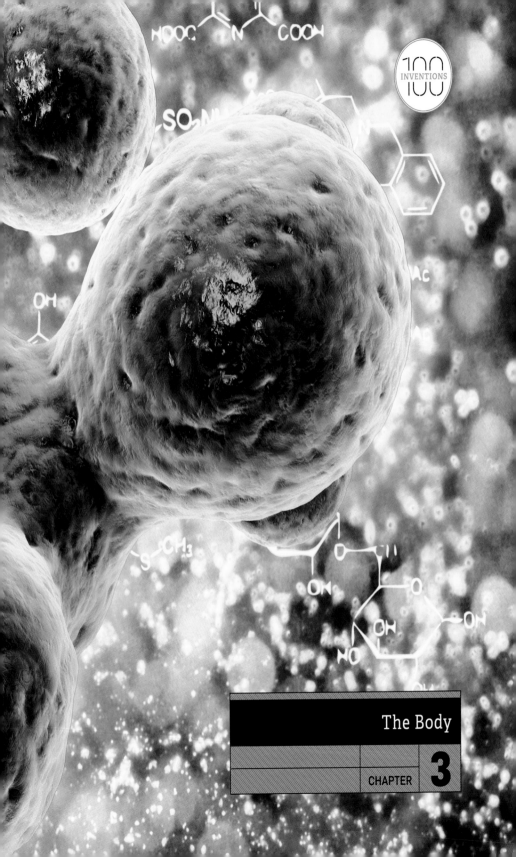

The Body

CHAPTER **3**

In Vitro Fertilization

The theory behind in vitro fertilization (IVF) sounds like science fiction—a story from the *Twilight Zone*, in which babies appear without active involvement by either parent. But in real life, in vitro fertilization (from the Latin word for "in glass," meaning "outside the body") has given thousands of families the gift of fertility.

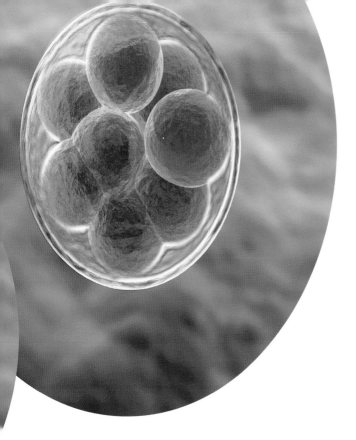

In vitro fertilization is costly and therefore reserved for patients who can afford it or have the insurance to cover the procedure. It's also a complicated process. First, a woman is given medication to help her body produce multiple eggs. A minor surgery follows to extract the eggs, and then they are mixed in a laboratory dish. The eggs are stored in an environmentally controlled chamber and, after as little as five days, a successful embryo will actively divide and be placed inside a woman's womb.

In 1944, John Rock and his research assistant Miriam Menkin produced the first successful "test-tube" fertilization. They did not attempt to place the fertilized egg in a woman, but their success generated a lot of publicity—mostly negative. Pope Pius XII condemned all fertilization occurring outside a woman's body, saying that couples who do so take "the Lord's work into their own hands." In Illinois in 1954, a court went as far as declaring that any babies born by artificial insemination would be legally illegitimate.

The media firestorm stoked the public's negative opinion of IVF. It wasn't until the US Ethics Advisory Board finally allowed federal funding and approval of IVF research, but by that time other countries were leading the way. In England, Robert Edwards and Patrick Steptoe attempted in vitro fertilization for John and Lesley Brown. Their fertilized egg was implanted in Lesley and successfully resulted in pregnancy. On July 25, 1978, the first test-tube baby—a healthy girl named Louise Brown—was born. Public opinion finally shifted in support of IVF, and universities and clinics have since scrambled to supply the increasingly growing demand.

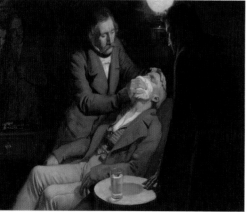

An illustration depicting the first use of anesthetic by Dr. William T. G. Morton during a dental surgery. Although others had experimented successfully with anesthetic on human beings before, Morton was the first to preserve the experience for public record by allowing observers to monitor the operation.

Anesthetic

The thought of being operated on while awake and fully cognizant of one's pain and suffering can make even the toughest customer cringe with fear. And yet, before 1848, the excruciating pain of surgical and dental procedures could be abated with nothing more than opium, alcohol, and perhaps a leather strap to bite on. The medical community experimented for decades to find a safe, effective solution without a whole lot of success.

In 1846, Dr. William T. G. Morton began working with an organic solvent, sulfuric ether, he had learned about from his chemistry professor at Harvard. Professor Charles Jackson had discussed how inhalation of the gas could render a person unconscious and numb. Morton began experimenting on himself and his pets with sulfuric ether fumes. Once he concluded the fumes were both relatively safe and reliable, he recruited a patient for surgery. Dr. Morton administered anesthesia while another surgeon operated in the surgical amphitheater of Massachusetts General Hospital in Boston. The surgery went off without a hitch. The patient remained unconscious during the procedure and felt no pain.

Early forms of anesthesia were usually a combination of inhaled ether and chloroform. A large part of Morton's achievement was owed to the ether inhaler he developed to dose the patients. To regulate inhalation depending on the patient's state of consciousness, he used a glass flask with a specially designed wooden mouthpiece. Today, the treatment includes nitrous oxide and derivatives of ether such as isoflurane, sevoflurane, and desflurane. Modern treatment is usually administered via needle and intravenous injection—although in some cases the drug is still inhaled.

In spite of centuries of successful usage, the explanation as to how and why anesthetics work remains a mystery. Scientists believe the gases dissolve portions of fat within brain cells that change cell activity and render the patient unconscious and pain-free—but they have yet to prove the theory. They do know that the effects of general anesthesia interrupt the function of the cerebral cortex, thalamus, reticular activating system, and spinal cord. Recent studies at Harvard Medical School, Weill Cornell Medical College, and the Massachusetts Institute of Technology suggest undergoing anesthesia is more similar to experiencing a coma than it is to deep sleep.

Conquering pain during surgical procedures was one of the greatest medical achievements of all time, giving humans the chance to sleep peacefully through operations big and small. Although there certainly are risks associated with anesthesia, the evolution of new and different medications has helped decrease complications for patients of every age.

Penicillin

Throughout most of human history, infectious diseases have killed more people than all wars combined. Until relatively recently, it was common for women to die from infections after childbirth and for children to die from infections before age five. Even a simple cut, if infected, could turn into a life-and-death struggle. Of the 620,000 soldiers who died in the US Civil War (1861–1865), more than two-thirds succumbed to infections, not combat. Most people seemed to accept that infection, illness, and untimely death were simply part of life.

The *Penicillium notatum* fungus produces the antibiotic penicillin.

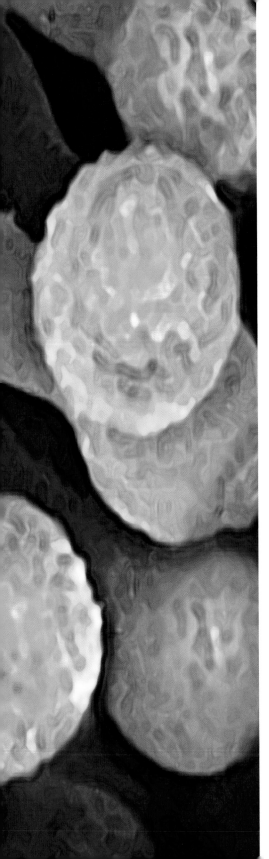

In the 1860s and 1870s, Louis Pasteur and others developed the "germ theory of disease," which explained that blood toxins produced by bacteria were the cause of many infectious diseases. The problem, the scientists realized, was finding a way to destroy bacteria before they could cause disease and death.

In 1928, Scottish bacteriologist Alexander Fleming made a breakthrough discovery. Growing a common mold—*Penicilium notatum*—in a laboratory culture, Fleming found it produced a substance that killed colonies of *Staphylococcus aureus* bacteria. He isolated the substance and named it penicillin. When Fleming published the results of his experiment, he noted the discovery might have great medical value if penicillin could be produced in large enough quantities.

Still, practical use of penicillin had to wait until the 1940s, when the manufacturing process was jointly invented by Howard Florey, an Australian pathologist, and Ernst Chain, a German-born biochemist. Finally, Fleming's discovery could be manufactured and distributed as a drug. In 1945, all three men shared the Nobel Prize in Medicine.

Today, penicillin is recognized as the first of a long line of life-saving antibiotics. According to some estimates, it's saved more than 82 million lives.

Brassiere

Although burned and maligned as a show of support for the women's rights movement in the 1960s, the bra was actually invented in the early 1900s to offer women freedom from uncomfortable, constricting corsets.

New York socialite and poet Mary Phelps Jacob was 19 years old in 1913 when she unwittingly revolutionized women's fashion after losing patience with her corset. The clever young debutante couldn't stop support rods in her corset from poking up from beneath the fabric of her evening gown. Ignoring fashion dictates of the day, Jacobs found two silk handkerchiefs and, with the assistance of her maid, sewed them together using pink ribbon and cord. The result was soft, lightweight, and liberating, offering women comfort in dress previously unattainable.

Friends took notice and Jacob began taking orders. Realizing the potential of her design, she patented what she called the Backless Brassiere in 1914 and began selling the garment under the name Caresse Crosby. Although it was not the first garment of its kind, it was the first brassiere, or bra, to be widely worn.

In the early 1920s, Jacob—discouraged by her husband at the time—decided not to pursue the business. She sold the patent to Warner Brothers Corset Company (now Warner's) for $1,500. Although the company eventually discontinued the design style of the handkerchief bra, it made millions from the patent, especially when the War Industries Board of World War I asked women to stop buying corsets in order to conserve metal for military production. According to the PBS series *Who Made America*, the movement to reappropriate steel used in corsets diverted 28,000 tons (25.4 million kg) of metal to the war effort—enough to build two battleships.

Russian immigrant Ida Rosenthal lifted the brassiere industry even higher in 1928 when her small New York-based company, Maidenform, introduced cup sizes and designs for different life stages. Rosenthal's A-B-Cs of bra sizing caught on like crazy: Maidenform sold 500,000 bras and a megabrand was born. In the 1930s, manufacturers added adjustable elastic straps, padded cups, and other improvements.

In 1977, Polly Smith and Lisa Lindahl's "jogbra" revolutionized the field for their increasingly active consumers. Throughout the following decades, new styles of brassieres have appeared, keeping pace with the latest fashions and women's needs.

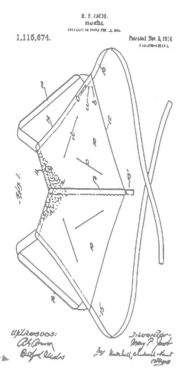

Kevlar

The thin, lightweight fiber called Kevlar is made up of a liquid crystalline polymer solution that is five times stronger than steel. Kevlar is resistant to wear, corrosion, and flames. It is used in skis, safety helmets, camping gear, suspension bridge cables, fiber optic cables, airplanes, automotive belts, and anything that calls for increased strength, reduced weight or extended wear.

But it is in bulletproof vests that Kevlar has made the biggest impact. It takes an enormous amount of energy to stretch the Kevlar's fibers due to the high tensile strength of its molecular structure. Bulletproof vests are made up of many layers of the twisting fibers, allowing them to absorb the impact of a bullet without penetration.

Kevlar was invented by Stephanie Kwolek while she was working for DuPont in the 1960s. DuPont then set about searching for a viable commercial application for the new crystalline polymer. The light weight and durability were at first used to reinforce radial tires, but a team of scientists soon discovered a myriad of other uses.

Most police agencies have adopted mandatory vest requirements, using Kevlar to protect police officers every day. Kwolek's invention has been more than just influential. "When you think about what she has done, it's incredible. There's literally thousands and thousands of people alive because of her," the former manager of the Kevlar Survivor's Club, Ron McBride, told *USA Today*.

Kwolek started as a chemist at DuPont in 1946 with just a bachelor's degree, replacing men who were serving in the military. She stands as the only female employee to be awarded DuPont's Lavoisier Medal, one of the few women to receive the National Medal of Technology, and one of a handful of women to be inducted into the National Inventors Hall of Fame. Stephanie Kwolek died in 2014 at age 90. In 2015, DuPont celebrated the 50th anniversary of Kevlar.

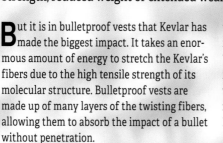

Jeans

Seen everywhere from the Paris runway to the Western ranch, blue jeans have been a clothing staple throughout the twentieth century. Jeans are made from denim, a material with origins in a French town called Nîmes (*de Nîmes* means "of Nîmes"). Denim pants, known to be extremely durable, had existed for many years before rivets were added—characteristic of what we now call "jeans."

I n the nineteenth century, denim pants were worn primarily by sailors and other workers, until a young, German immigrant named Levi Strauss improved upon them. Levi followed the California gold rush to San Francisco and established Levi Strauss & Co. to sell cloth. Nearby, a tailor named Jacob Davis learned to place metal rivets in pants where they were most likely to rip from wear and tear. In 1878, Strauss partnered with Davis, and they received a patent to create a new and longer-lasting pair of pants. For the next 30 years, these "waist overalls" remained a staple of the Western labor force. Even after the company's patent ran out, many people still referred to the pants as Levi's.

As news spread about the durability of Levi's, their popularity grew. When cowboys adopted the working man's pants, consumers soon associated denim jeans with the heroic image of the American West. Young military men brought the pants to World War II. After the war, jeans became a symbol of rebellion, personified by bad-boy celebrities like actor James Dean, and young people claimed the style as their own.

Often deemed too casual by adult authorities, denim jeans were forbidden in places like church, school, and offices. The popularity and impact of jeans spread around the world. According to Levi Strauss & Co., British teenagers would swarm the docks before ships could even unload the new shipment of jeans. Asian markets were just as strong.

Despite their European origins and worldwide popularity, however, jeans were always seen as quintessentially American. Over the years, the cut and color of jeans have changed, and the high-fashion denim market has exploded, but even modern technology cannot replace the classic design. Jeans are one of the few items that just never seem to go out of fashion.

IN THE 1960S, BABY BOOMERS BEGAN CALLING THE PANTS "JEANS" AND THEY BECAME THE SYMBOL OF A NEW GENERATION.

Vaccination

Vaccination is the medical practice of injecting a patient with weak bacteria or viruses. Once in the body, they trigger the immune system to attack and kill the pathogen, which is too faint to cause disease. The desired effect? To sensitize the body's antibody-producing cells so they have "memory" of the vaccine—and can recognize the disease and destroy it, should it enter the body again.

Today, children and adults are routinely vaccinated for a host of diseases. Vaccines have been developed for mumps, measles, typhoid, cholera, plague, tuberculosis, tetanus, influenza, yellow fever, and typhus—all major killers of humans in the past.

Although there are indications that the ancient Chinese were aware of the principle of vaccination, the first modern use is attributed to the British physician Edward Jenner. During the 1760s, Jenner noticed that dairy workers never seemed to contract smallpox, the highly contagious disease that caused the deaths of 20 to 60 percent of infected adults and more than 80 percent of infected children. But he noted that dairy workers did contract cowpox, a very mild form of the disease. By 1796, Jenner was experimenting with this lesser pox, administering it to patients with the hope that he was providing immunity from the more deadly smallpox. He took pus from the hand of a milkmaid and scratched it into the arm of an eight-year-old boy. Six weeks later, he exposed the boy to smallpox, observing that the boy did not contract the disease.

Perhaps the most notable vaccination program in recent history was the development and use of the polio vaccine. In the 1950s, summer was a time of fear and anxiety for many parents because children by the thousands would come down with the crippling disease poliomyelitis, or polio, commonly transmitted through swimming holes or poorly chlorinated pools. The burden of fear was lifted forever in 1955 when it was announced that Dr. Jonas Salk had developed a vaccine against the disease.

Today, in countries that use the vaccine, polio has been virtually eliminated. When he died at age 80 in 1995, Dr. Salk was working on a vaccine for AIDS.

Dr. Jonas Salk began trials of his polio vaccine in 1954.

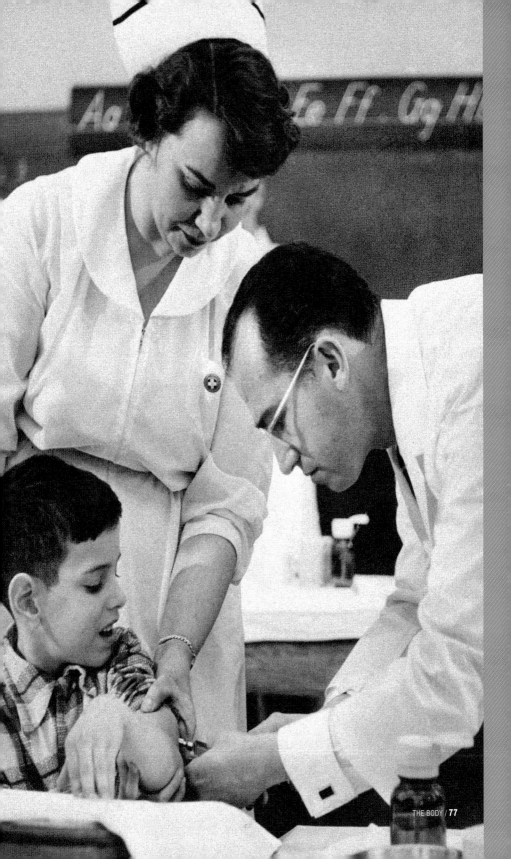

The Pill

In 1957, the US Food and Drug Administration approved the production and sale of the first oral contraceptive for women, known as "the pill."

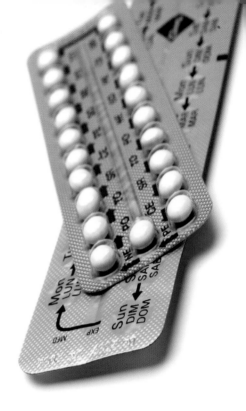

T he medication, containing a combination of the hormones estrogen and progestin, is designed to suppress ovulation by preventing the ovaries from releasing an egg. In addition, the pills, taken daily, cause changes in cervical mucus and the lining of the uterus, making it difficult for sperm to reach an egg (thus preventing fertilization) and keeping any fertilized eggs from attaching to the uterine wall and developing.

The fight for oral contraception for women began in 1951, when women's rights activist Margaret Sanger persuaded endocrinologist Gregory Pincus to develop a pill that women could take to prevent pregnancy. At that time, conservative public opinion condemned birth control for women. The powerful Catholic Church warned that using artificial means of preventing pregnancy was a sin. It was against the law in most states to even sell contraceptives.

In 1944, Dr. Pincus opened the Worcester Foundation for Experimental Biology in Massachusetts. His work focused on the role of hormones in reproduction. A year later, Pincus met obstetrician John Rock, who had also been working on developing chemical contraception for women, and they combined their efforts. Sanger also recruited Katherine McCormick, a biologist, women's right advocate, and heiress, to fund the mission.

In 1954, the scientists surreptitiously tested birth control pills on a sampling of women. The medication worked to prevent pregnancy.

With public pressure mounting and religious and conservative forces working against him, Dr. Pincus felt compelled to reveal his work and declare success.

In a sly marketing move, the scientists and the G.D. Searle pharmaceutical company decided to ask the FDA to approve the pill not as a contraceptive but instead as a method for regulating irregular, severe menstrual cycles. A warning label on the bottle, however, read, "Warning: This pill will likely prevent pregnancy." Suddenly, an inordinately high number of women reported irregular cycles to their physicians.

By 1960, the pill was approved by the FDA for use as a contraceptive, and within two years more than 1.2 million women had prescriptions. By 1965, 6.5 million American women were on the pill, and today, more than 10 million women are. The pill has contributed to lower birth rates, fewer women dying in childbirth, less unwanted conception, and the addition of millions of women to the workforce.

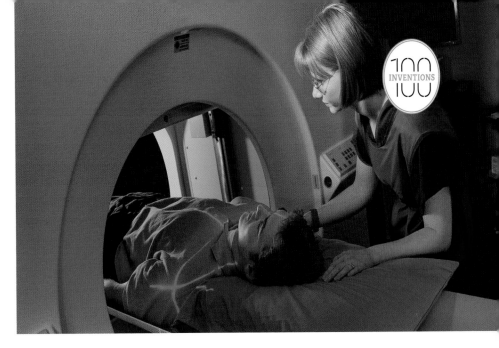

CT Scan

Until 1972, doctors had two ways to look inside patients: with a scalpel or with an X-ray that revealed bone structure but couldn't provide conclusive analysis of soft tissue and organs. The invention of the CT scan—computerized tomography scan or computerized axial tomography (CAT) scan—by British engineer Godfrey Hounsfield and South African–born physicist Allan M. Cormack allowed doctors to view internal organs and tissue without performing invasive, possibly life-threatening surgery.

Hounsfield and Cormack's machine merged computer technology with X-rays to provide a detailed, cross-sectioned image inside the body. For the first time, doctors could see the size, shape, and position of organs, tissues, and tumors. The CT scan was especially helpful in assessing the brain because it provided a picture of soft tissue in 100 times more detail and information than a regular X-ray.

The revolutionary imaging tool works by taking multiple X-ray images (slices) at different angles of the body area being scanned, then digitally stitching them into a three-dimensional view via computer. The first patient to undergo Hounsfield's CT scan was suspected of having a brain lesion, and the new technology confirmed clearly a dark, circular cyst.

The invention was groundbreaking; however, the first CT scan could only accommodate a person's head, arm, or leg when inserted into the machine. In 1973, Robert S. Ledley, a Georgetown University physicist, introduced the first full-body scanner, which he called the automatic computerized transverse axial (ACTA) scanner. Today's CT scan patients lie on a platform that moves through a machine with a hole in the middle. An X-ray tube rotates around the hole as the patient moves through it. One full turn of the X-ray tube is one slice of the body. Faster scanning machines take more slices per second, reducing the time of CT scans to less than 20 minutes.

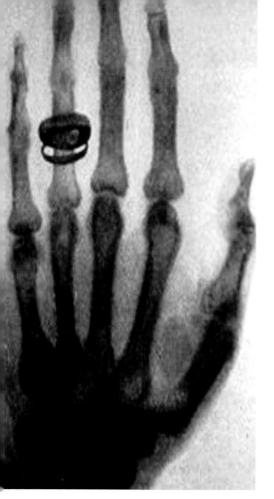

X-ray

An X-ray is, in essence, a look deep inside something. It is a photographic image produced by electromagnetic waves able to pass through opaque materials.

In 1895, German physicist Wilhelm Conrad Röntgen was investigating a cathode-ray tube. He found that the negative and positive electrons within the tube produced a fluorescent glow on a screen across the room of his lab when an electrical current was applied. Further experiments led him to discover that this glow, or ray, could travel through various barriers, including heavy black paper, aluminum, and even the plaster walls of his lab. Finally, a piece of lead blocked the ray, but a chance projection of part of his own hand holding the lead piece on the screen revealed that the ray could pass through human flesh and illuminate bones inside the body. Shortly after, Röntgen published a paper outlining an experiment: Replacing the screen with photographic paper, Röntgen produced an X-ray (dubbed "X" for "unknown") picture of the bones in his wife's hand, her wedding ring also appearing in the image. One year later, the Glasgow Royal Infirmary set up a radiology department, and the field of medicine was transformed.

In 1903, W.D. Coolidge, an inventor at General Electric Research Lab, improved upon the X-ray by creating high-vacuum tubes that could withstand higher charges of energy and enable longer emission of X-rays, thus creating a more powerful product. He developed small, portable X-ray machines and applied the new power for industrial purposes. Coolidge also invented a sealed tube that held a high-wattage transformer, enabling X-ray radiation to penetrate teeth.

Today we understand that X-rays are electromagnetic energy waves similar to light rays and that they have some harmful effects. It wasn't until the 1950s that physicians understood the risks of radiation associated with X-rays. In those days, X-ray machines emitted a dose of radiation 1,500 times greater than today's machines. After doctors made the correlation between X-rays, burns, skin damage, and skin cancers, they began using X-rays more judiciously and while wearing protective gear.

X-rays are now standard operating procedure in the medical profession and security fields throughout the world. The technology has paved the way for other imaging systems, including radar, CAT scans, and MRI.

Pacemaker

Heart disease is the number one cause of death in the United States; approximately 1 million men and women die of it every year.

Heart diseases can cause arrhythmias, which are problems with the rate of a person's heartbeat—likely caused by aging. Pacemakers were invented to treat arrhythmia, and this is how they work: Sensors, called electrodes, detect activity in the heart and send information through wires to a tiny implanted computer. If the rhythm is abnormal, the computer directs a generator to send electrical pulses to the heart via wires that run from the computer through the vein. Then electrodes attached to the right ventricle stimulate the heart muscle. Some pacemakers also attach to the right atrium and the left ventricle, depending on a patient's diagnosis. Modern pacemakers can also detect other data such as breathing and blood temperature, giving the computer information that allows it to adjust the rhythm depending on the patient's activity level.

About the size of a wristwatch, a modern titanium pacemaker can last for many years. Doctors and innovators continue to perfect the life-saving device, sending shock waves through the world of medicine.

It all started in the 1930s with better understanding of the heart and experimentation with electrotherapy. These rudimentary pacemakers were large, bulky devices that drew current from a wall socket to shock the patient's heart into a regular rhythm. They were used on the operating table during surgery and could not travel with the patient after discharge from the hospital.

The first wearable pacemaker, designed by the American engineer Earl Bakken, was worn around the neck, but common infections made it risky. Scientists searched for a way to implant the device into a patient's chest, just below the collarbone, to minimize risk, and a breakthrough eventually came by accident. While building a device to record the heart's rhythm, Wilson Greatbatch, an assistant professor of electrical engineering at the University of Buffalo, reached into a box and pulled out the wrong size transistor. He noticed the transistor emitted a pulse that could mimic a beating heart. After conducting several experiments on dogs, Greatbatch received a patent in 1959 and began implanting the device inside human patients. At first, the new device wasn't perfect. Body fluids permeated the electrical system, causing it to fail. Greatbatch then developed a long-life, corrosion-free, lithium-iodine battery to power the pacemaker. Now, patients undergo a short surgical procedure to receive an implantable pacemaker that can last for 10 years.

Electrocardiogram
(ECG, EKG)

The human heart operates as a two-stage electrical pump and produces electrical currents. This groundbreaking information was originally revealed in 1889 by British scientist Augustus Waller, who demonstrated by recording the electrical activity of his dog's heart.

Dutch doctor Willem Einthoven witnessed the demonstration and, expanding upon Waller's premise, began further research to capture and record the electrical currents of the heart. He wanted to measure the electrical activity as the small current, or "shock," moved rapidly down the heart, then back up again, making the muscle contract and pump blood.

In 1901, Einthoven constructed a string galvanometer that was sensitive enough to measure the heart's electrical signals from outside the body. By 1903, he had perfected what we now recognize as the electrocardiograph (ECG, or EKG, from the German *Elektrokardiogramm*) machine.

Einthoven's invention used thin pieces of wire that were connected to the patient's chest with electrodes and attached to electromagnets. In order for the machine to work, the patient's hands had to be submerged in a saltwater bath to conduct the necessary electrical impulses. The resulting electromagnetic field made the wire vibrate almost imperceptibly in response to the heartbeat, but it was enough. Using film and a light directed on the wire, the machine accurately recorded the strength and rate of the heartbeat in millivolts and graphed the positive and negative deflections of the EKG curve. The printed results—an electrocardiogram—are now standard documents in hospitals worldwide.

The first EKG machine weighed 600 pounds (272 kg) and required five technicians to operate. However, in spite of its mass and labor-intensive processes, the invention was a triumph. Considered extremely precise, the technology enabled doctors to proactively diagnose cardiac abnormalities and disease, thus preventing heart attacks.

The medical breakthrough earned Einthoven a Nobel Prize in 1924. Two years later, he was awarded a patent for the wireless signal he developed as the foundation for his EKG monitoring technology.

Hypodermic Needle

True, hypodermic needles can and do cause a pinprick of pain, but they improve your health and alleviate even greater pain than they inflict.

A hypodermic needle is a hollow steel tube with a gauge, or diameter, measured in millimeters. Commonl sizes range from 7-gauge (the largest) to 33-gauge (the smallest). A 21-gauge needle is often used for drawing small amounts of blood for testing, while a 16- or 17-gauge needle is best for blood donation. The tip of the needle is beveled to create a sharp point that easily penetrates the skin.

The hypodermic needle fits into the open end of a syringe, which operates like a basic pump, or piston, consisting of a plunger that fits tightly inside a tube. The plunger can be drawn upward to suck up blood or liquid, thus filling the tube, or pushed down, to release a liquid or gas through the needle for an injection or infusion. Syringes, once made of steel, are now made of glass or disposable clear plastic that enables medical professionals to see inside. The barrel of the tube features graduated markings to measure the volume of fluid contained in the syringe.

"Hypodermic," a word of Greek origin, gets its name from hypo, meaning "under," and derma, meaning "skin." In 1853, Dr. Alexander Wood, the secretary of the Royal College of Physicians in Edinburgh, Scotland, performed the first subcutaneous injection to alleviate pain using a regular syringe and a hollow needle. Wood's experiment was the first time a doctor was able to inject medicine—in this case, morphine—directly into the bloodstream.

Several years later, lauded New York City–based surgeon William Halstead applied the new technology to inject a small amount of liquid cocaine into the root of a sensory nerve, successfully numbing the area during oral surgery.

The concept and technology of the hypodermic needle has remained mostly unchanged since its introduction more than 150 years ago. Tweaks to the design have included tailoring the needle size and length for specific medical uses, as well as advancements in disposable versions. Today, hypodermic needles provide the vehicle for treatments such as vaccines, prescription drugs, and blood transfusions that would have been impossible to administer otherwise.

In the future, advancements in the technology of hypodermic injections might also make them painless. In 2013, Mark Prausnitz, an American chemical engineer, introduced his prototype of the Microneedle. Similar to the nicotine patch, the Microneedle consists of 400 microscopic, silicon-based needles that are so tiny they administer medicine through the skin and into the bloodstream without triggering the nerve cells that signal pain back to the brain. Although the Microneedle is not yet available to the public, it looks like your annual flu shot might get a whole lot more enticing—and your reason for skipping it a lot less convincing.

RUBBER, RAINCOAT,
ARMOR, LOVE GLOVE, LOVE
SOCK, FRENCH LETTER—
ALL ARE NICKNAMES
FOR AN INVENTION THAT
HAS BROUGHT IMMENSE
JOY AND LIFE-SAVING
PROTECTION TO MANY.

Condom

For millions, the image of a condom aging away inside a wallet or of a youth nervously approaching a pharmacy counter to buy protection is familiar. Purchasing a condom, a barrier method of contraception, is often a rite of passage for young people, but it is a valued means of preventing pregnancy at any age. Condoms are also used as protection against sexually transmitted diseases and HIV-related illnesses. Condoms are most commonly made of rubber or latex and come in a variety of sizes. Some have spermicide or lubrication additives. Statistics indicate they have a 98 percent success rate at preventing pregnancy, when used correctly.

The invention and patenting of vulcanized rubber in 1844 by Charles Goodyear paved the way for modern, synthetic condoms.

Thanks to the new material, a relatively cheap form of protection became available. Over the next several decades, advancements in condom design and materials, including the development of latex and spermicide, made usage widespread and significantly reduced incidence of disease and unwanted conception.

In the 1980s, after a decline in popularity due to the advent of oral birth control for women, condoms once again gained global attention for their recommended role in the fight against the virus that causes AIDS. In 1987, the US surgeon general advocated the use of condoms as an important preventive measure against the spread of the disease, and the importance and influence of the personal "armor" were restored.

Stethoscope

Many people have heard their stomach growling or listened to their heartbeat in the middle of the night. But few know that inside the human body is a cacophony of sounds—from the gurgle of the intestines to the whisper of the lungs and the rush of the arteries.

Doctors can learn about a patient's health from the sounds they hear through a telescope—Greek for *stethos*, meaning "chest," and *skopein*, meaning "to explore." Modern stethoscopes feature a round chest piece containing a hollow cup (bell) with a plastic disk, or diaphragm, inside it. When the piece is placed on the patient's chest, body sounds vibrate the diaphragm, creating sound waves that travel up hollow rubber tubes to the listener's ears. The bell transmits low-frequency sounds, while the diaphragm transmits higher-frequency sounds.

René Laennec invented the stethoscope in France in 1816. Reportedly, while walking in Paris, Laennec saw two children sending signals to each other using a long piece of solid wood and a pin. With an ear to one end, the child received an amplified sound of the pin scratching the opposite end of the stick. After much experimentation, Laennec came up with the first stethoscope. It consisted of a wooden tube and was connected to one ear only. The tool was very similar to the ear trumpet, a device used by the hard-of-hearing to listen to conversations and the rest of the world.

Flexible-tube stethoscopes for one ear arrived in 1840. They were called "snake ear trumpets." In 1851, Irish physician Arthur Leared invented a binaural (two-eared) stethoscope, which greatly improved the ability of a doctor to hear internal bodily sounds.

Today, physicians use many types of stethoscopes. The acoustic stethoscope is the most familiar, but there are also electronic stethoscopes (stethophones) that electronically amplify body sounds. They use a PC-based software that converts the sound into visual graphs that can be transmitted for remote diagnosis.

The invention of the stethoscope marked a major step in the redefinition of disease. Formerly identified as a bundle of symptoms, disease in the current sense is considered a bodily problem even if there are no noticeable symptoms. Using a stethoscope, a doctor can quickly tell the health of the lungs, heart, stomach, and intestines, even if the patient notices no pain.

Pasteurization

Wine and beer drinkers deserve hearty thanks for making our milk supply safe. If that sounds counterintuitive, then consider the story of Louis Pasteur and the development of pasteurization, or what the FDA defines as "a process that kills harmful bacteria by heating [the substance] to a specific temperature for a set period of time."

Louis Pasteur's work in germ theory led to the invention of pasteurization. Pasteur, a chemist and microbiologist in France, discovered that bacteria came from the environment. While working to help the French wine industry in the 1850s, he proved that bacteria were responsible for souring wine and beer. After several experiments, he realized that harmful bacteria could be removed by boiling and then cooling the liquids. He later applied that concept to dairy products, and today milk is the main recipient of the process he that named "pasteurization."

Routine pasteurization of milk to reduce bacterial contamination and illness began in the United States in the 1920s. The milk is heated just long enough to destroy germs but not the important nutrients. Before pasteurization, untold numbers of people died from ingesting milk that was more than a few hours old. Pasteurization and refrigeration greatly extended the product's shelf life.

Some critics believe that Pasteur created an obsession with eliminating bacteria, even though 90 percent of the human body contains trillions of bacteria. But especially on today's large-scale dairy farms, pasteurization ensures food safety.

Pasteurization tanks at a dairy. In the United States, unpasteurized milk is illegal in many states.

While many think that Dolly, shown here, is the first cloned specimen, cloning (the duplication of organisms or cells) has occurred for thousands of years on a horticultural level.

Cloning

In the late 1800s, scientists began experimenting and debating whether the genetic information of an animal cell would diminish with each cell division, and whether there was enough DNA inside the resulting split cells to generate new specimens.

In the early 1900s, German embryologist Hans Spemann split a two-cell salamander embryo, which then grew into two complete organisms, proving that cells retain the genetic info required for life as they divide.

In 1914, Spemann transferred the nucleus of one cell into an egg without a nucleus, performing the first successful nuclear transfer experiment. He earned the Nobel Prize in Medicine in 1935 for his work, which provided the foundation for the study of cloning. Over the next three decades, scientific advancements in the field of molecular biology increased public awareness of cloning.

In 1984, using an advanced version of the kind of nuclear transfer first tested by Spemann, Danish scientist Steen Willadsen successfully cloned a sheep from embryonic cells. It was

Writer Christen Brownlee explains in the article "Nuclear Transfer: Bringing In the Clones":

"NUCLEAR TRANSFER IS A TWO-PART PROCESS: FIRST, SCIENTISTS REMOVE THE NUCLEUS FROM AN EGG, AND SECOND, THEY REPLACE IT WITH THE NUCLEUS OF AN OLDER DONOR CELL. A NEW CLONE— A GENETIC COPY OF THE DONOR— FORMS WHEN THE EGG STARTS TO DIVIDE."

Ian Wilmut, right, one of the scientists who produced Dolly and Polly.

the first substantiated case of cloning a mammal.

Two years later, Willadsen cloned a cow using differentiated cells taken from week-old embryos. The same year, scientists Neal First, Randal Prather, and Willard Eyestone at the University of Wisconsin also cloned a cow from embryonic cells.

Up to this point, experimentation had centered on embryonic cells. In 1996, however, after 276 unsuccessful attempts, Ian Wilmut and Keith Campbell at the Roslin Institute in Scotland made a groundbreaking leap: They cloned the first animal from adult cells. Dolly the sheep was born on July 5, 1996. The little lamb made history, the cover of *Time* magazine, and a lot of people nervous. Replicating an animal from adult cells had opened a universe of possibilities and

perhaps perils. Many feared the ethical implications of cloning adult cells and worried that cloning humans was just a few years away.

In 1997, the United States declared a five-year moratorium on the appropriation of federal funds for human cloning. Wilmut and Campbell didn't live in the United States, however, and their experimentation continued. That same year, the pair cloned a Dorset lamb named Polly from skin cells genetically altered to contain a human gene.

In spite of these successes, scientists remained skeptical about the breakthrough without proof the animals had been recreated from differentiated cells (specialized cells from a specific kind of tissue) and not, accidentally, stem cells— that is, undifferentiated cells. This question was resolved

in 2002 when scientists at the Whitehead Institute for Biomedical Research at the Massachusetts Institute of Technology successfully cloned mice from cells specific to the immune system. Since the cells contained a built-in marker system, scientists were able to distinguish these cells from existing stem cells, thus determining that it is possible to produce a clone using the nucleus of a fully differentiated cell.

Today, in spite of relatively limited success rates, scientists envision one day using cloning processes to reproduce animals genetically engineered with organs that are suitable for human transplantation; to help endangered species avoid extinction—or even to revive an already extinct species; and to harvest stem cells from embryos in order to develop treatments for various diseases and save lives.

Things That Go

CHAPTER 4

Automobile

MORE THAN 100,000 PATENTS WERE FILED LEADING UP TO THE INVENTION OF CARS AS WE KNOW THEM TODAY.

For many, the credit for designing the first car in the race to the patent office goes to Karl Friedrich Benz. On January 29, 1886, Benz filed a patent for a vehicle with three large, wire-spoke wheels, an integrated chassis with an open carriage seat, and a gasoline-powered internal-combustion engine. The single-cylinder, 2.5-horsepower car could reach a top speed of 25 miles per hour (40 kmh).

On that same day in 1886 in another German town, unbeknownst to Benz, a different set of engineers, Gottlieb Daimler and Wilhelm Maybach, filed their own patent. The Daimler-Maybach vehicle incorporated the body of a four-wheeled, horse-drawn carriage fitted with what they called the Grandfather Clock Engine—considered the precursor of modern gasoline engines. Daimler and Maybach's engine, which is what they were really patenting that day, featured a single horizontal cylinder, air cooling, a large, cast-iron flywheel, a hot-tube ignition system, and a 600 rpm running speed that outpaced previous engines and boasted 1.1 horsepower. In 1889, the duo put the engine into a vehicle of their own design and showcased it in Paris.

In the meantime, Benz used his accumulating patents for speed regulation systems, spark plugs, a carburetor, a clutch, a gear shift, and a radiator to engineer the first commercial vehicle, which he called the Patent Motorwagen No. 3.

In 1887, it was displayed at the World's Fair in Paris and became the first production automobile. The gasoline-powered vehicle featured Benz's four-stroke engine set between the rear wheels. Karl Benz's company, Benz & Cie.,

eventually became the car manufacturer we know today as Mercedes-Benz.

Since Benz's time, cars have become equipped with air conditioning, radios, safety belts, entertainment systems, and navigation systems, among other things. The proliferation of automobiles throughout the world has led to complex infrastructures of roads, bridges, and highways. The automobile has spurred businesses as varied as construction, manufacturing, energy, food and beverage, and advertising and marketing.

Automobiles continue to evolve. The shadow of climate change has led to clean energy technologies and the development of vehicles that accommodate different fuel types. Electric hybrid cars are gaining in popularity. Tesla Motors' luxury electric car has breathed new life into a niche thought to be a fad.

It's not difficult to see the future of the automobile, either. Autonomous vehicles (driverless cars that are already in prototype) utilize remote sensing technology and are poised to change our "car culture" once again.

A luxury electric car manufactured by Tesla Motors plugged into a streetside charging station.

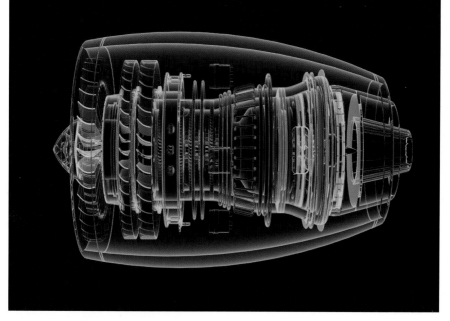

Jet Engine

Could Sir Isaac Newton, theorizing the laws of physics in the 1700s, ever have envisioned a machine as powerful as a jet engine?

Believe it or not, the mechanics behind the jet engine are based on Newton's third law, which says that for every action, there is an equal and opposite reaction.

A jet engine, also called a gas turbine, is described by NASA as follows: "The engine sucks air in at the front with a fan. A compressor raises the pressure of the air. The compressor is made with many blades attached to a shaft. The blades spin at high speed and compress or squeeze the air. The compressed air is then sprayed with fuel and an electric spark lights the mixture. The burning

gases expand and blast out through the nozzle at the back of the engine. As the jets of gas shoot backward, the engine and the aircraft are thrust forward." The propulsion of the engine is an equal and opposite reaction to the gas jets' backward thrust—Newton's law in action. The technology would eventually allow planes to fly faster and higher than ever before.

As a cadet in Great Britain's Royal Air Force (RAF), Frank Whittle, the son of a mechanic, developed the thesis that if planes were going to fly farther and faster, they would have to fly

at a higher altitude, where air resistance was lower. But the conventional piston engines and propellers in use in the 1920s wouldn't do. Whittle drew up plans to enclose a high-powered fan inside the fuselage that would be powered by a gas turbine, eliminating the need for pistons and propellers. In 1941, Whittle tested a prototype, and the jet engine soared into the skies on May 15.

Jet engine technology not only changed the way we fly, but also the way we live. Today, engineers are creating more fuel-efficient engines and new designs that reduce noise.

I do not know what I may appear to the world, but to myself I seem to have been only like a boy playing on the seashore, and diverting myself in now and then finding a smoother pebble or a prettier shell than ordinary, whilst the great ocean of truth lay all undiscovered before me.

— ISAAC NEWTON

F-35 Lightning

Stealth Aircraft

Cloaking technology sounds like the stuff of video games—in which technology renders your fictional army invisible. Today's engineers use their knowledge of light and electromagnetic waves to develop such technology for real.

F-35 Lightning

Stealth technology, or stealth aircraft, represents a major victory in military innovation. Most aircraft leave a "radar signature" when they fly, even at high altitudes. It was discovered in the 1970s that this signature could be calculated using a mathematical model. Innovators also learned that faceted surfaces deflected radar energy—unlike the flat features of traditional fighter planes.

The year 1975 saw the first prototype of a stealth aircraft. It was dubbed "The Hopeless Diamond" for its shape—and the doubt many had that the aircraft could even fly. (It was also a pun on the world's most expensive gem, the Hope Diamond.) Once scientists understood how to control this type of craft, they devised new designs that improved the aerodynamics of the faceted surfaces, reduced the amount of heat radiating from the planes, and coated them in radar-absorbent materials.

Stealth aircraft debuted in combat in 1989 during the US invasion of Panama, when the F-117 Nighthawk triumphantly bombed airfields and enemy targets, able to fly into the war zone undetected by radar. Continued improvement in stealth aircraft design has allowed the United States to fly planes in every major conflict since Panama, including the Gulf Wars, conflicts in Afghanistan and Iraq, and the 2011 invasion of Libya. The F-22 Raptor, the B-2 Spirit, and the F-35 Lightning are actively deployed by the US military at a cost of billions.

In the future, the producers of these "cloaked" aircraft plan to develop stealth payloads that increase the amount of weaponry the planes can carry. They're also researching ways to reduce the atmospheric disturbance created when stealth aircraft pass by, an effect that can be picked up by passive monitoring systems and make stealth aircraft vulnerable.

B-2 Spirit

Wheel

Many inventions lay claim to being the most important of their time. But few have altered the course of civilization as much as the wheel.

Simply put, a wheel is a circular object with a hole in the center, designed to rotate on a fixed axle. Historians debate whether the wheel was invented in a single place and then spread to other regions around the globe, or if it came into use at the same time in various places. There is evidence to support the origin of the wheel in both Mesopotamia (present-day Iraq) and the Eurasian steppes.

Surprisingly, the wheel did not start off as a means of transportation. Most historians believe that the first wheels were for making pottery, based on a 5,500-year-old Mesopotamian wheel. Farming, boats, musical instruments, rope, and weaving were all common approximately 3500 BCE when the wheel was used to move people and goods from place to place.

Humans first developed the sled as a means of carrying heavy loads and later placed it atop round logs, making the load easier to pull. The wheelbarrow evolved from this apparatus: The round logs developed grooves, reducing the friction from the sled on top, making the turning motion easier, and the sled gave way to the wheelbarrow with moving axles and wheels.

During the following period, known as the Bronze Age (ca. 3000 BCE), new metal tools allowed craftsmen to create fixed axles sized with great precision that fit into the smooth, round hole at the center of the wheel, maintaining the right amount of friction and support to allow the wheel to move easily and rapidly. Although the evolution of the wheel's design was complete, transportation was still mainly relegated to camels, since they traveled more easily over the sand and uneven roads of the desert region.

The wheel later became important to farming and other growing trades, serving as a catalyst for migration and eventually the Industrial Revolution. Few inventions from that time are still in use today and certainly none are as ubiquitous as the wheel.

"The wheel is come full circle." — WILLIAM SHAKESPEARE

Shipping Container

Stacked seven stories high along the side of commercial docks or on ships slowly making their way across the oceans of the world, shipping containers evolved from an idea known as "intermodalism." According to the World Shipping Organization, intermodalism is "a system that is based on the theory that efficiency will be vastly improved when the same container, with the same cargo, can be transported with minimum interruption via different transport modes from an initial place of receipt to a final delivery point many miles away. That means the containers would move seamlessly between ships, trucks, and trains."

Before the development of shipping containers, loading and unloading goods was a labor-intensive business. It would take hours for scores of men to unload cargo from the hold of a ship, stack it on docks or load it into wagons, and later trucks, in order for merchandise to reach its final destination. Once it did arrive, more manpower was devoted to unloading. Thousands of years went by with only small improvements in the storage and transfer of goods. Then, during World War II, the US government established a uniform-sized crate for all goods shipped overseas to the troops. This improved upon storage limitations and made the often difficult practice of rooting around cargo holds quicker and safer. It was Malcom P. McLean, the owner of a trucking and steamship company, who realized he could put the trailer of one of his trucks directly onto a ship. In 1956, McLean's *Ideal X*, a World War II tanker ship converted for commercial use, traveled from the port at Newark, New Jersey, to the Port of Houston carrying 58 shipping containers. Other companies soon followed suit. In 1957, McLean's Sea-Land company launched its first ship designed and dedicated for transporting containers. Rail cars called flatcars were also built to accommodate containers.

By the early 1960s, shipping containers had become an international business. Made of corrugated aluminum or steel, containers are designed in a variety of ways, depending upon the cargo they hold. Thanks to global efforts to standardize the size of containers, today the two most frequently used sizes are the 20-foot (6-m) equivalent unit (TEU) and the 40-foot (12-m) equivalent unit (FEU). Standard sizes means the boxes can be stacked efficiently, and ships can be built to specifications that accommodate the containers. Specific numbers assigned to them aid in tracking containers around the world. The International Maritime Organization regulates standards concerning construction of containers, what and how goods are packed in a container, weight of the loads, and security.

Today, retired containers are repurposed as offices, swimming pools, and even homes.

Compass

If you've ever felt disoriented on the water or lost your way in the woods, you can appreciate the value of the compass. Instead of navigating by landmarks or being guided by the stars, you can find your way with this tool, which dates to the fourth century and reliably points north.

The Chinese are credited with building the earliest compasses with lodestone, a magnetic form of the mineral magnetite, which reacts consistently with Earth's magnetic field and exhibits natural north-south polarity.

Today's magnetic compass works off that same concept: a small lightweight magnet called a needle sits on a frictionless bearing and reacts to Earth's magnetic field. The relatively weak magnetic pull created by the North and South Poles causes the tip of the needle to reliably point north. It works because scientists theorize that there is a magnetic core consisting mostly of molten iron at the center of our planet.

This core creates radiating convection heat that moves in a rotational pattern as Earth turns on its axis, producing a low-level magnetic field. The theory, however, has not yet been proven definitively.

Over centuries, the compass was developed into the small, portable device we recognize today. Small as it is, its impact on history has been invaluable. Since the most efficient way to move goods and supplies was over water, being able to safely and

accurately navigate allowed countries to generate wealth through trade. In addition, seafarers were able to explore increasingly distant shores, learn new cultures, and establish colonies.

The technology of the early compasses also inspired the study of magnetism and laid the foundation for work in electrostatics. And resulting discoveries in electromagnetism opened the door wide for telecommunications.

The word "sonar" is an acronym for sound, navigation, and ranging.

Sonar

Throughout much of history, what lies beneath the ocean—from sea monsters to submarines—has been a guessing game. Ships—from Roman triremes to the *Titanic*—simply had no good way to see what lay ahead of them under the ocean's surface. There were no "eyes and ears" able to see and hear underwater until the invention of sonar.

Sonar uses sound propagation to determine what objects are underwater, including other vessels. Today, sonar consists of two types: active sonar ("eyes") that emits pulses of sounds and listens for echoes when the pulses hit objects, and passive sonar ("ears") that listens for sounds made by other ships. Much as a bat does, sonar uses echolocation—bouncing sound off objects to determine their distance and size.

The invention of sonar was spurred by the "unsinkable" *Titanic*'s catastrophic collision with an iceberg in the north Atlantic in 1912. If the *Titanic* had been equipped with sonar, the ship's crew would have detected the iceberg in time. Just one month after the disaster, the world's first patent for an underwater echo-ranging device was filed by British meteorologist Lewis Richardson. In 1913, German physicist Alexander Behm obtained a patent for a similar model.

During World War I, the need to detect German submarines, which were devastating British sea trade, mandated the development of echolocation gadgets. By mid-1917, the anti-submarine division of the British Naval Staff had produced a practical and workable underwater sound-detection machine.

During the 1930s, US engineers began to use the term "sonar," which they coined as the equivalent of "radar," for their systems.

Modern submarines use sonar for navigation underwater. Fishing boats use it to detect and track schools of fish. Oceanographers use it to map the ocean floor. For many years, the United States has operated the Integrated Undersea Surveillance System, a large set of passive sonar arrays at various points in the world's oceans designed to give early warning of enemy submarines headed toward our shores. Other nations are believed to have implemented similar systems.

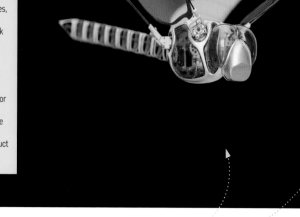

ALL KINDS OF DRONES

Drones are now available in all shapes and sizes, depending on the type of work for which they are intended. Drones built to resemble dragonflies or birds could be used for eavesdropping. Larger UAVs are used to drop bombs or conduct surveillance.

Drone

Drones, or unmanned aerial vehicles (UAVs), are aircraft piloted by remote control, or, more frequently, determined by preprogrammed flight paths. Drones are primarily used by the military for surveillance or equipped with missiles for precision strikes. However, as drone technology progresses, the list of commercial applications is growing.

Drone research began as early as World War I and continued through World War II, but early programs had little success. The allure and practicality were obvious—fewer pilot casualties—but the failure rates left much of the research on the drawing board for years. Surveillance drones became popular in the 1960s, when intelligence-gathering agencies relied on simple mechanisms equipped with cameras. In the 1990s, arming drones became a priority for the military once again. Today, a pilot can sit safely in a building in one country while directing a

drone to surveil an area in another country or to launch a strike on a particular region or even an individual.

Drones are made of lightweight materials that can withstand high altitudes. However, drones are still strong enough to carry a payload of missiles or imaging systems or perhaps, in the future, even personal packages. Most drones are equipped with cameras, GPS, and sensor systems.

Today, simple drones can be made by hobbyists with kits. While little regulation currently exists regarding the civilian use of drones, as

new purposes
arise for them,
so does controversy
over privacy issues and the
legislation that governs their
usage. Especially as drone
technology grows more
compact and even camouflaged,
some are concerned about
surveillance becoming an even
greater part of modern life.

The nonmilitary uses for
drones have expanded to
include forest fire detection,
conservation, local law
enforcement, filmmaking,
mapping, traffic control, and
scientific research. Some
people also foresee a role for
drones in disaster relief and
construction.

Locomotive

Picture the classic image of a steam engine locomotive flying across the Western landscape, transporting freight or bringing passengers to new destinations.

Railroad cars, pulled by an engine that converts power and transmits it to driving wheels, were first created in 1829 and ran only on steam power until World War II. In the 1950s, the diesel engine replaced many of the archaic steam engines, and diesel power still propels most trains today due to its low operating costs, lower energy use, and higher speeds.

The transcontinental railroad's appeal was that it connected the coasts of a large continent, compressing the trip by horse-drawn coach from a three-month ordeal to a convenient 10 days aboard a fashionable Pullman sleeping car. It revolutionized personal travel, but it also allowed for the efficient transit of goods, allowing for the development of the American West.

Today, most high-speed passenger locomotives are powered by overhead wires that pass electricity. Even still, the use of locomotives in the United States has steeply declined, as commuters, voyagers, and traders alike transitioned from passenger and freight service by train to personal automobiles, corporate trucks, and sprawling interstates. However, trains still move bulk shipments of materials like coal.

Advocates hope to see the return of passenger trains, especially as global warming feeds the desire to cut back on the number of cars on the road.

LOCOMOTION NO. 1

Riding on the success of the steam engine, the first "traveling engine" was developed by George Stephenson in 1814. Combining his knowledge of tramways with the new steam engine, Stephenson built the *Blucher* to haul coal. Moving at 4 miles per hour (6.4 kmh), the engine was slower than a horse but could carry 30 tons (27,215.5 kg). Although people marveled at the new mode of transportation, the *Blucher* was plagued with repeated breakdowns and problems, inspiring Stephenson to improve the design. The first public railway opened in England in 1825. Traveling along those cast-iron rails was the *Locomotion*, driven by Stephenson himself. The distance between the rails was set at 4 feet, 8 inches (1.2 m, 20 cm), creating the standard for railways to come.

Guided Missile

Precision-guided bombs play a decisive role in modern warfare, allowing countries to invade others with minimal risk. Miniature computers guide the bomb or missile toward its target, using feedback systems to change the course if necessary.

When a fighter plane releases a bomb, the plane uses its infrared radar to view the target and directs a laser beam that locks on the target. The bomb's light-sensing nose divides the view into quadrants and measures the intensity of the laser light on the target. If all four quadrants have the same amount, the bomb is on track; if not, the computer makes a correction. Seconds later, the target is destroyed.

Guided missiles first emerged during World War II, when Germany experimented with Fritz-X, a bomb directed by radio signals to hit ships at sea. The US Air Force also experimented with different guided weapons and made several successful attacks. However, the early prototypes had little

practical effect during the war. For the remainder of the twentieth century, the US military attempted to fine-tune different missiles, succeeding in developing weapons that could find their target and elude detection.

During the 1990 Gulf War, the United States severely weakened the Iraqi army while suffering comparably few casualties. America's accurate bombs easily found small targets like tanks and personnel carriers, with one military spokesman estimating that less than one-tenth of 1 percent of all guided missiles hit civilian areas, according to the *New York Times*. The guided missiles were even able to hit planes or helicopters, moving targets considered impossible before.

Many military experts

declared this a new era of warfare, in which guided missiles could nullify the previous advantages held by tanks or large numbers of infantry. The accuracy of the guided missile has come to creates immense fear in targets—and equal confidence in those who wield them.

The first remote-controlled device was built by Nikola Tesla, the Croatian-born engineer and inventor. His idea was soon applied to guided missiles, using instructions from a wireless remote-control transmitter that could detonate an explosive charge at a safe distance.

A fighter plane flies above the payload it has just released, keeping track of the missile's path to its intended target.

H.L. HUNLEY

In 1775, American David Bushnell built the *Turtle*, a hand-powered underwater device. In 1864, the Confederate navy's *H.L. Hunley* became the first military submarine to sink an enemy vessel, the Union's sloop-of-war USS *Housatonic*.

Submarine

People have always been fascinated by submarines, from Captain Nemo's submarine *Nautilus* in *Twenty Thousand Leagues Under the Sea* to the Beatles' "Yellow Submarine" to today's powerful, sleek modern vessels. Whether it's an antique diesel-powered World War I sub or a modern nuclear one, all submarines are based on a simple principle: the ability to adjust buoyancy.

In all submarines, buoyancy depends on the boat's ballast tanks, which are found between the sub's inner and outer hulls. A submarine resting on the ocean's surface has positive buoyancy, which means the sub is less dense than the water around it, causing it to float. To achieve positive buoyancy, the ballast tanks must be mainly full of air, not water. To submerge, the submarine must become denser than the water, or achieve negative buoyancy. The crew opens vents on the top of the ballast tanks, allowing seawater to enter and forcing air out, and the sub begins to sink.

Adjusting the water-to-air ratio in the ballast tanks controls the exact depth of a submarine. Neutral buoyancy, meaning that the density of the submarine equals the density of the amount of water it displaces, allows the sub to remain in a static position.

Submarines first made a significant military impact in World War I when German U-boats used torpedoes to sink ships in the Atlantic Ocean. And by the end of World War II, Germany used U-boats again to sink almost 3,000 Allied ships. Submarines, though only about 2 percent of the US Navy during World War II, are credited with destroying more than 30 percent of the Imperial Japanese Navy.

Today, nuclear power is used in all large submarines, but due to the high cost and large size of nuclear reactors, smaller submarines still use diesel-electric propulsion. Besides torpedoes, modern submarines also carry ballistic missiles and cruise missiles, both of which can be launched when the sub is underwater.

Saturn V was the most massive rocket ever built. It was 363 feet (110.6 m) tall, about the height of a 36-story building. Fully fueled for lift-off, it weighed 6.2 million pounds (2.8 million kg).

FLY ME TO THE MOON, LET ME PLAY AMONG THE STARS, LET ME SEE WHAT SPRING IS LIKE ON JUPITER AND MARS…

Saturn V

Saturn V streaking across the sky after liftoff

When the jazz song "Fly Me to the Moon" was written in 1954, it described an impossible journey. By the time Frank Sinatra recorded it in 1964, it had become the informal theme song of the US Apollo space program designed to land a man on the moon. As most people know, the historic landing took place on July 20, 1969, when astronaut Neil Armstrong stepped onto lunar soil—the first human to walk on the moon.

The craft that Armstrong stepped out of was part of Saturn V, a remarkable rocket that made the moon voyage possible. Saturn V was a three-stage liquid-fueled launch vehicle, the largest ever built. It was the result of years of planning and engineering headed by NASA rocket scientists Werner von Braun and Arthur Rudolph at the Marshall Space Flight Center in Huntsville, Alabama.

Saturn V, a "heavy lift vehicle" designed to carry astronauts to the moon and back, functioned in three stages. The first stage was powered by five massive liquid-propellant rocket engines. The engines used a kerosene-based RP (rocket propellant) fuel injected with liquid oxygen in the thrust chamber to produce a powerful controlled explosion. Saturn V's first-stage engines were the most powerful liquid-propellant engines ever built.

When the first stage burned away, the second stage took over, also powered by five liquid-propellant engines that used liquid oxygen as an oxidizer, with liquid hydrogen this time as the fuel. Stage two put Saturn V into orbit around Earth. From there, Saturn V's third stage, also powered by liquid hydrogen and liquid oxygen, took the astronauts to the moon. Once shut down, the third stage was designed to be restarted for the trip back to Earth.

Saturn V was launched 13 times from the Kennedy Space Center in Florida with no loss of crew or payload. It still holds the record for the heaviest payload ever launched into low Earth orbit: 260,000 pounds (117,934 kg). It propelled a total of 24 astronauts to the Moon, three of them twice, from December 1968 through December 1972.

Radar

The term "radar" is an acronym for "radio detection and ranging." Radar is the system in which radio waves are bounced off objects. The reflected wave is able to indicate the distance and direction of an object and the speed at which it is traveling. Unlike many other inventions, no single person invented radar. It is the result of the combined scientific discoveries of many individuals.

In 1867, the Scottish scientist James Clerk Maxwell predicted the existence of radio waves—electromagnetic radiation with wavelengths longer than that of infrared light. Proof, however, had to wait until 1887, when German physicist Heinrich Hertz demonstrated that radio waves could be created in laboratory experiments.

Many subsequent inventions made use of these "Hertzian" waves to transfer information through space, and this ability of radio waves to transmit information would lead to the invention of the radio. Hertz also discovered that transmitted radio waves bounced off metal objects, which eventually brought the development of radar in the early twentieth century, when engineers first developed a device that could make use of radio waves' deflection.

In 1903, the German engineer Christian Hülsmeyer developed the first radar transmitter, which he called a "Telemobiloscope." When it sent a radio signal toward an object, the signal bounced back, allowing Hülsmeyer to calculate the distance from the machine to the object. The Telemobiloscope was first used as part of a simple ship detection system intended to help ships avoid collisions in thick fog. Numerous similar systems, which provided directional information about objects over short ranges, were developed over the next two decades.

Between 1934 and 1939, eight nations developed Hülsmeyer's system independently, and in great secrecy as its potential in wartime became apparent. In England, the birth of modern radar is memorialized in a plaque honoring scientists Robert Watson Watt and Arnold Wilkins, who "showed for the first time in Britain that aircraft could be detected by bouncing radio waves off them ... It was this invention, more than any other, that saved the RAF (Royal Air Force) from defeat in the 1940 Battle of Britain." The acronym "radar" itself was coined in 1939 by the US Signal Corps as it worked to develop its own systems for the Navy.

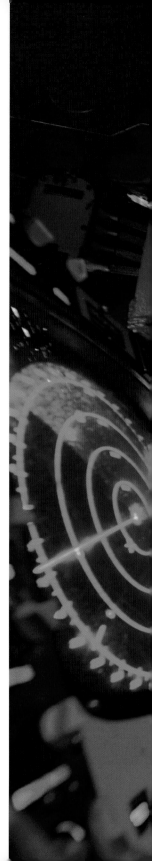

Far beneath the surface of the ocean, the crew of a nuclear submarine monitors the dark waters around them. Radar alerts them to any objects in their midst. High above the clouds, aircraft employ radar to monitor other planes and, in wartime, missiles aimed in their direction. On the ground, your car beeps as you back out of your driveway into traffic, alerting you to oncoming vehicles or objects blocking your path. We can thank radar technology for keeping us safe in both mundane and high-risk circumstances.

Making Something Out of Nothing

CHAPTER 5

What Ford accomplished was significantly reduced labor turnover, a new market for his cars, and a production system that would be emulated around the world.

Moving Assembly Line

In 1907, Henry Ford declared that he would soon make automobile transportation affordable for all people. In order to make the cars less expensive, he had to reduce production costs, so he began looking at other industries to study their processes. Ford identified four elements of production that would help his company achieve its goal: using interchangeable parts, creating a division of labor, providing a continuous flow of goods, and minimizing wasted effort.

Ford and his team worked for five years to develop a smoothly operating system. In order to improve workflow, Ford took cues from Chicago's meatpacking houses and the conveyor belt technology of canneries, breweries, flour mills, and industrial bakeries. The idea was for the parts to come to the workers, not the other way around. Ford and his team divided the process of making the Model T into 84 steps. The time and motion required for each step was calculated to determine the speed of the process. This process revolutionized man-ufacturing, becoming the first moving assembly line.

In December 1913, a Model T rolled off the first moving-chassis assembly line used for major manufacturing. Production time was reduced from more than 12 hours per car to merely 2 hours and 30 minutes. As a result, Ford was able to lower prices and sell more cars. Ford's own employees, however, still couldn't afford to buy them. He believed that the people making the cars would also make the best and most loyal customers, so he more than doubled their wages to $5 per day—which was considered an excellent rate in that era. In addition, he changed shifts from nine hours a day to eight. He could now operate three shifts a day instead of two.

Today, although moving assembly lines remain an integral part of production across all industries, the need for speed and reduced costs continues to drive development. As a result, moving assembly lines are becoming increasingly automated as factory employees are taken out of the equation and replaced with robotic technology.

There are no big problems,
there are just a lot of little problems.

— HENRY FORD

Sometimes called anti-friction bearings, ball bearings are small, perfectly shaped, (usually) metallic or ceramic spheres used to reduce friction between shafts and axles—basically any machine that employs a rotary motion.

The small moving spheres reduce wear and tear (i.e., constant stress) on component pieces by substituting a sliding motion between moving parts.

Think about what would happen if you tried to "skate" across a wood floor wearing socks, then if you tried the same thing across a wood floor covered with marbles, and you'll get an idea of how ball bearings help things move and reduce the friction and wear of surface against surface.

An antique invention, ball bearings appear in some of our most modern inventions, including NASA Exploration Rovers roaming Mars.

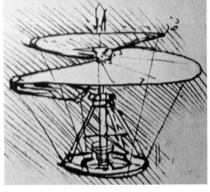

Ball Bearing

Ball bearings don't immediately spring to mind as one of the world's most influential inventions—until you stop to think what life would be like without them.

The little round balls that are virtually unnoticed in roller skates, watches, garage door openers, video game controllers, skateboards, bicycles, guitars, blenders, washing machines, microwave ovens, computer hard drives, fishing reels, and hot tubs (to name just a few!) are the humble heroes of everyday life. And on a grander scale, major projects (including the Mars Rover and the Hubble Telescope also make use of ball bearings).

Although the concept was used as early as the Roman Empire in 40 CE (archaeologists discovered a lazy Susan–style serving platter with ball bearings), Leonardo da Vinci's designs were the first written records to incorporate them. It was inventor Philip Vaughan, a carriage maker in Carmarthen, Wales, however, who received the first patent in 1794 and put ball bearings to good use in carriage axles.

Ball bearings' ability to move easily in a rotary or linear fashion has made them indispensable. In fact, since these bits of hardware are a crucial component of countless items, it is reported that Great Britain's Royal Air Force often bombed Germany's ball bearing factories during World War II in a strategic attempt to handicap its enemy where it really hurt.

Screw

Sometimes the phrase "If it ain't broke, don't fix it" doesn't mean the object in question can't be improved; such is the case of the screw. The screw is defined by Merriam-Webster as a "rod-shaped piece with a spiral groove and a slotted or recessed head designed to be inserted...by rotating (as with a screwdriver) and used for fastening pieces of solid material together."

Although the basic concept of the screw hasn't changed since it was first conceived by Greek mathematician and inventor Archimedes in the third century BCE, it has evolved.

The simple technology first appeared in hand-operated machines used for raising water for irrigation and removing bilge water from ships. Based on that early model, Pythagorean philosopher Archytas of Tarentum incorporated screw thread technology for pressing everything from water to clothing, wine, and olive oil around 400 BCE. These first screws were cut by hand from wood.

Upon the invention in the mid-eighteenth century of the lathe's semiautomatic screw drive (with its ability to move longitudinally), metal screws became objects of uniform precision. The lathe-cut screws were used to construct steam engines and to create new tool-making machines. The use of screws in survey instruments facilitated the construction of canals, roads, and bridges.

Although the applications for the building component were limitless, lack of standardization in thread design made it impossible to use screws interchangeably. In 1841, English mechanical engineer and inventor Joseph Whitworth solved this problem. After collecting and studying sample screws from British workshops, he proposed two rules: Thread flanks should be standardized at 55 degrees, and the number of threads per inch should be made regular according to the pitch diameter. The directives, which became the British Standard Whitworth (BSW), unified British industries, and the interchangeability that resulted created an engineering revolution.

Later modifications led to an International Organization for Standardization (ISO) edict, which stated that the thread measurements should be produced in metric. Today, screws are manufactured with both metric and inch threads for builders in the United States and the rest of the world.

The use of screws has allowed for more durable structures everywhere, and they are considered one of the most important technological advancements in history. Today, screws hold our lives together in every way imaginable, from our electronic devices to modes of transportation and beyond—a pretty big job for such a tiny little tool.

Nail

Early nails were made by a blacksmith using a square iron rod. The blacksmith would heat the rod in a forge and then hammer all four sides of the softened end to form a point. He would then form the nail's flat head by placing it on an anvil and striking it with a hammer. In addition to the nails themselves, blacksmiths would spend arduous hours creating the tiny but expensive tools necessary for construction. Luckily, by the 1800s, machines were invented to make the process easier. While nails had been crucial in construction for ages, the invention of the nail machine is more significant, as it made the tool available in large numbers at a cheaper price.

It is unclear exactly when the very first nail was formed to ease the burden of hewing, notching, and pegging each board of a building. Bronze nails found by archaeologists date to 3000 BCE, and nails are referenced in the Bible, most notably in the crucifixion of Christ. The Romans were the first to mass-produce nails, and their hand-wrought, iron versions continued unchanged for thousands of years.

The invention of the nail machine in the late 1700s relieved blacksmiths from the tedious work of making thousands of nails. The machine, which created a nail by shearing it off an iron bar like a guillotine, was first developed by inventor Jeremiah Wilkinson. Further inventions perfected the process, and the new machine was able to make 100 nails per minute. The invention proved fortuitous as the Industrial Revolution came to depend on nail factories.

But in this case, technology has not made nails better—only cheaper. In the 1900s, round steel wire replaced iron as the material of choice. And by 1913, the new steel wires, which could be created at a fraction of the cost, replaced a staggering 90 percent of nails in the United States. These modern steel-wire nails have cylindrical shanks that easily slide into wood, but they have only a quarter of the holding power of iron nails.

What the new nails may lack in strength, they certainly make up for in bulk. Manufacturers compensate for their weakness by packaging them in boxes of 300 or more, and everyone from master builders to hobbyists is now able to purchase these nails for an affordable price.

Hidden in everything from our furniture to the house that shelters us, nails have been a critical part of construction for centuries.

3-D Printing

The manufacturing industry is on the brink of change, as three-dimensional printing technology moves out of the novelty phase and into the consumer's hands.

Already a staple of engineering labs, 3-D print shops are appearing in malls and shopping districts, and hardware and software are available for home use.

Three-dimensional printing is made possible by using a manufacturing technique called additive process, which builds layer upon layer to create a 3-D object. A computer controls the process, turning the printer into a type of robot that can create medical implants, shoes, auto parts, clocks, toys…and eventually just about anything.

A printed 3-D object always starts with a computer-generated design made using CAD (computer-aided design) software. Another software program then slices the object into individual two-dimensional layers and uploads them

Today, 3-D printers for the public are just for fun—video gamers on Minecraft can print out the worlds they've created and kids can make toys—but as the technology improves, it is likely to change how we live.

Loading....

to the 3-D printer. The printer creates the object by reading and producing hundreds, sometimes thousands, of these layers, stacking them until an object emerges.

The most common type of 3-D printing is the fused deposition modeling process (FDM). In this process, a machine within the printer dispenses material (plastic filament or metal wire) into an object and a support structure that will be disposed of once the object is complete. An extrusion nozzle, moving horizontally and vertically according to software that conveys the design of the object, regulates the flow of material. The nozzle heats the plastic or metal, enabling each layer to be molded; the layers harden when cooled.

3-D printing is already being used in unique ways. In 2014, astronauts working aboard the International Space Station found they needed a socket wrench to perform some basic tasks. Luckily, the astronauts had a 3-D printer. NASA emailed them a CAD model, and the astronauts then printed the 20 separate parts and assembled the wrench in space.

The film industry is also getting in on the fun: In the production of the James Bond movie *Skyfall,* for instance, a 3-D model of a vintage Aston Martin was created for the sole purpose of being blown up (rather than destroying a priceless vehicle). Cameras, musical instruments, and medical models also make the list of popular 3-D printed objects—and someday, food, bodily organs, and housing on Mars may make the list, too.

Experts expect 3-D printing to transform many industries, but none more than manufacturing. Customization and small outputs will be more common and the need for large manufacturing centers eliminated. In the future, all households may have a 3-D printer, inspiring entrepreneurs in small, homespun businesses or enabling consumers to create their own spare parts for domestic objects.

Windmill

Human beings have always looked for ways to harness the forces of nature in order to improve their own lives. The windmill is a prime example of that desire.

Early windmills were most commonly used to pump water or to mill grain. Windmills have been found in Persia and China dating back to 1219 CE, but they differ in design from the commonly known windmills of the West. In the early designs, blades or sails (usually consisting of a wooden or reed lattice on which cloth was stretched) rotated horizontally while fixed on a vertical axis.

The windmill structure that is more familiar to the Western world was designed by the Dutch in the late fourteenth century and is known as the tower mill design. A tower mill is divided into individual floors, each story devoted to a different task, such as storing grain, separating the wheat from the chaff, and milling grain. The sails move on a vertical plane, mounted on a post, or "buck," of a brick or stone building. The advantage of a vertical mill is that the face of the blades can be rotated to take advantage of whichever direction wind is coming from. At one time, there were more than 200,000 windmills throughout Europe.

Windmills made their American debut in the Midwest as a method for pumping water in the 1850s. Small systems with lightweight steel blades, millions of these structures could be found throughout the heartland well into the 1900s.

Windmills remained a prominent source of power until the early nineteenth century saw the development of the steam engine, and they declined in popularity even further when the internal combustion engine rose to prominence. Today, the expertise gleaned over hundreds of years has been reapplied in the global push for greener, renewable energy, giving us the wind turbine—a sleek, modern variation on the windmill that transforms wind energy into electricity.

A windmill transforms wind into rotational energy, which can then be used to power machines.

Cement

Cement is not exciting. In fact, a popular analogy to describe a really boring activity is watching cement dry. However, there is greatness behind the powdery substance that has been used as the basis of concrete for centuries. The Roman Colosseum could not have been made without early interpretations of cement. The Hoover Dam, the largest concrete project in the world, stands as a modern testament to its brilliance, as do millions of miles of roadways and sidewalks and countless skyscraper and bridges.

NYC'S BROOKLYN BRIDGE

Common materials used to manufacture cement include limestone, shells, and chalk or marl, combined with shale, clay, slate, blast furnace slag, silica sand, and iron ore. When baked at high temperatures, these ingredients result in a chemical combination of calcium, silicon, aluminum, iron, and other ingredients. This rocklike substance, called clinker, composed of what look like gray balls the size of marbles, is then ground into the fine powder we recognize as cement.

Bricklayer and contractor Joseph Aspdin of Leeds, England, was not looking for fame or a place in the history books when he began seeking a substance that would bind bricks together in a predictable, dependable fashion. However, after some experimentation, that is exactly what he got. Aspdin hit upon a strong, binding, waterproof building material by pulverizing limestone and clay together, then heating the mixture in a kiln and grinding the resulting clinkers into powder. The balance between calcium, iron, silicon, and aluminum produced the substance he desired.

Aspdin patented his discovery, which he named Portland cement after the color of local Portland stones, in 1824. When the cement was used by local engineers Isambard Brunel and Joseph Bazalgette, it not only made Aspdin famous, but also changed the course of history and the world we live in along the way. Brunel used the new material as a foundation in the building of the Thames River tunnel in the 1830s and other railway tunnels, while Bazalgette used it to build the London sewer system (1859–1867).

Since then, cement has played an important role in every major building, tunnel, bridge, dam, and sprawling bit of infrastructure that we rely on in our everyday lives. Turns out, boring is actually better—especially when it means that the world we've built stays standing up.

A Bessemer converter removes impurities from iron by blowing air through the molten metal. The oxidizing process is performed in an oval-shaped steel container lined with clay or the mineral dolomite.

Steel

"Steel" today means much more than just the name of a widely used metal construction material. It is a synonym for strength—for example, Superman is called "the Man of Steel," and the expression "steel yourself" encourages people to summon up their internal strength for a challenge.

To make steel, iron ore is first mined from the ground, then smelted under high heat in a blast furnace to remove impurities. Blast furnaces are huge steel cauldrons lined with heat-resistant bricks. The temperature at the bottom of the blast furnace reaches more than 3,000 degrees Fahrenheit (1,649 degrees Celsius). The impurities, or slag, float on the top of the molten iron ore and drain off, leaving pig iron, or pure molten iron. Steelmakers then add carbon for flexibility and other alloys to make steel for different industrial uses.

Steel has been around since antiquity. The earliest known production occurred at an archaeological site that flourished more than 4,000 years ago in what is now Turkey. In artifacts from ancient times, steel appears primarily as a material in weapons, as it helped metalworkers create swords and other tools that were lighter, stronger, and more flexible than those made from iron alone. For example, the Roman army carried steel swords, and the legendary swords used by Japanese Samurai warriors were also handcrafted out of steel.

Modern steelmaking began with the introduction of Henry Bessemer's "Bessemer process" in 1855. Bessemer's method, still used today, allowed steelmakers to produce steel cheaply in large quantities.

Nuclear Reactor

When scientists first discovered nuclear fission, the process that provides power for nuclear reactors, they focused their efforts on creating the atomic bomb but soon discovered fission's potential as a source of energy. Atoms, the building blocks of matter, have a nucleus filled with protons and neutrons held together by energy. Certain isotopes, like uranium-235, can be split and will release their energy as heat. Some neutrons are released with the heat and may hit other atoms, which also split, creating more fission in a chain reaction. Under the right conditions in a nuclear reactor, a continuous chain reaction occurs, creating a great deal of heat. The heat is converted to steam, which turns a turbine and a generator, producing electricity. Unlike steam power plants heated by coal, oil, or gas, nuclear power plants can generate a cleaner and more efficient source of energy.

A German chemist named Martin Klaproth first discovered uranium in 1789. A century later, famed scientists Pierre and Marie Curie coined the name "radioactivity," also known as nuclear decay, and scientists struggled to learn more about atoms and nuclear arrangement. When the first atom was split, scientists confirmed Einstein's theory about the relationship between mass and energy, sparking a flurry of activity in laboratories. The first controlled and self-sustaining nuclear reaction was achieved at the University of Chicago in 1942, and three years later the atomic bomb put a decisive end to World War II. After the war, plans shifted to commercialize nuclear fission as power. In 1955, the first reactor produced a usable amount of electricity from nuclear energy in Idaho. Since then, nuclear energy has been developed as a viable source of power, but safety has remained a controversial issue.

In 1986, a nuclear disaster occurred in Chernobyl, Ukraine. Four reactors overheated, and the resulting explosion released radioactive particles into the atmosphere over the European continent. Because of the accidents in Chernobyl and, more recently, in Fukushima, Japan, many people fear the negative risks of nuclear reactors. Although the potential for catastrophe is always there, nuclear energy remains a cleaner alternative to burning fossil fuels. Some people, however, believe there are better energy sources available. Mark Jacobson, professor of civil and environmental engineering at Stanford University, told NPR that nuclear power plants are costly and don't compare to renewable energy, such as solar power and wind turbines:

"IF YOU WANTED TO POWER THE ENTIRE WORLD ON NUCLEAR, YOU'D NEED ABOUT 17,000 LARGE NUCLEAR POWER PLANTS, EACH 850 MEGAWATTS. AND WE ONLY HAVE 400 TODAY."

Nonetheless, nuclear energy helps slow the progress of global warming and exists as a major source of power for cities around the world.

Nuclear power plants hold great promise—and also great danger. Top: Tihange, Belgium. Middle: Fukushima, Japan. Bottom: A village near Chernobyl in the Ukraine, now abandoned.

Steel Skyscraper

From a distance, it's easy to spot skyscrapers: very tall buildings that seem to pierce the clouds, dominating the skylines of London, New York, Shanghai, Tokyo, Sao Paulo, and a host of other cities around the globe. To what do we owe these modern, soaring views? Steel.

New skyscrapers seem to go up—and up—every week. Yet barely 100 years ago, there were no skyscrapers anywhere on Earth. Although definitions vary, the term "skyscraper" was first applied to buildings at least 10 stories high in the late 1800s.

Why did skyscrapers suddenly appear in a number of cities? The answer is steel-frame construction. Instead of using masonry (stone on stone), builders began to use steel to make a skeleton frame. Because steel was becoming more plentiful and because steel beams linked together provided a very strong bond, buildings could be raised higher and higher into the sky. Steel frames also allowed for large windows in each story, as the frame—not the glass—bore all the weight of the building. Other practical improvements also enabled builders to erect taller and taller buildings. Until the 1800s, for instance, buildings of more than six stories were rare because no one wanted to climb great numbers of stairs, and water pressure was typically insufficient to supply running water above 164 feet (50 m). The elevator solved the stairs problem, and improvements in hydraulic engineering solved the water issue.

The first steel-frame skyscraper was the Home Insurance Building erected in Chicago in 1885. Today, vast improvements in steel construction and design have allowed architects and engineers to build taller and taller skyscrapers. The Burj Khalifa building in Dubai rises 2,722 feet (830 m) into the sky and has 163 stories. It is the tallest man-made structure in the world.

Another steel skyscraper under construction is Saudi Arabia's Kingdo Tower, which is planned to rise more than 3,000 feet (914 m) above the city of Jeddah when it is completed (sometime before 2020).

Hydraulic Fracturing (Fracking)

The process of fracking requires natural gas and oil companies to drill vertical wells 7,000 feet (2,133 m)—about the height of six Empire State Buildings stacked top to bottom—into the ground to access large, subterranean formations of shale, called "plays." The goal is to mine the rocky reservoirs of natural gas and oil (hydrocarbons) trapped within the pores of the soft, sedimentary rock.

The drilled holes, called wellbores, are 12½ inches (31.75 cm) in diameter, lined with steel casing, and sheathed in cement. Once a wellbore reaches the depth of the play, the pipe takes a right or left turn (known as the kickoff point) and begins to travel horizontally. The Environmental Protection Agency (EPA) says the length of the horizontal piping can range from 1,000 to 6,000 feet (305–1,828 m). These horizontal pipes are finely perforated and act like sieves. When a fluid solution of water, sand, and chemicals (such as those found in detergents, disinfectants, and household cleaners) is blasted through the perforated pipes at high pressure, the shale fractures and releases hydrocarbons. Sand and additives in the fluid (such as ceramic pellets or small incompressible particles) hold open the fissures, and the gas and oil are forced up to the surface by internal pressure. There they are separated from the wastewater and stored.

The resurfacing of the fluid, called the "flowback," contains the original solution plus naturally occurring elements such as

WHAT THE FRACK?

Although forms of hydraulic fracturing, commonly referred to as fracking, have been used in the United States for more than 60 years, it is only within the past two decades that the technology and controversy surrounding the practice have really heated up.

brines, metals, radionuclides, and other hydrocarbons.

Fracking allows natural gas and petroleum producers to mine resources on a commercial level at a cost that enables both competitive consumer pricing and profit. It has revolutionized the mining industry and put the United States on par with Saudi Arabia in oil production. In fact, in 2013, the United States produced more oil than Saudi Arabia. Online news outlet Slate reported, "It's all about fracking. As the data for oil production shows, in 2013, the United States produced 7.44 million barrels of crude oil per day, the highest level since 1989, and up 49 percent since 2008. When we take into account liquid fuels produced from natural gas, America's production stands at about 11 million barrels per day and rising." In the near future, and with the addition of tens of thousands of new fracking wells proposed by 2020, the United States may in fact take the lead.

Critics of the technology, however, fear the cost of such a win. Concerns about drinking water contamination, spills, air pollution, and increased earthquake activity caused by fracking practices have triggered intense debate. The US Department of Energy has vowed to investigate the safety and processes of fracking, and companies such as Halliburton are promising to reduce risks of chemical exposure with newly designed fluids and technology to alleviate health and environmental concerns. Many people, however, remain wary.

Groundwater

Shale

FOR NOW, THE DEBATE, LIKE OUR INSATIABLE NEED FOR ENERGY, RAGES ON.

Bedrock

> "I KNOW NOT WITH WHAT WEAPONS WORLD WAR III WILL BE FOUGHT, BUT WORLD WAR IV WILL BE FOUGHT WITH STICKS AND STONES."
> — ALBERT EINSTEIN

Atomic Bomb

On December 21, 1938, nine months before the declaration of World War II, German radiochemists Otto Hahn and Fritz Strassmann were working near Berlin when a radioactive experiment yielded an unexpected marker for a new kind of nuclear reaction. Richard Rhodes, Pulitzer Prize–winning author of *The Making of the Atomic Bomb*, describes the discovery this way in his paper "The Atomic Bomb and Its Consequences": "The new reaction, converting a small amount of matter into energy, was fiercely exothermic, 10 million times as much energy coming out as the neutrons carried in. Physicists had known for forty years, ever since the discovery of radioactivity, that enormous energy was locked up in the atom. Here at last was a way to release it." The mystery of nuclear fission had been revealed.

Nuclear fission is the exothermic reaction that occurs when a large nucleus splits into two smaller nuclei, releasing a tremendous burst of energy. It produces both kinetic energy and electro-magnetic radiation. When harnessed by man, nuclear fission using uranium-235 and plutonium-239 creates a sustainable chain reaction that can produce energy at a controlled rate in a nuclear reactor—or at an explosive, uncontrolled rate in a nucle-ar weapon.

In 1941, President Franklin D. Roosevelt authorized a full-scale Anglo-American nuclear weapons program. Dubbed the Manhattan Project, the mission of this top-secret military operation was to weaponize the science of nuclear fission. Headed by US physicist Robert Oppenheimer and General Leslie R. Groves, the Manhattan Project created alliances between leaders in science, academia, industry, and government and utilized resources in 38 states.

Oppenheimer recruited some of the world's top scientists, including Albert Einstein, Enrico Fermi, and Leó Szilárd, to collaborate in a secret laboratory in Los Alamos, New Mexico, where the first atomic bombs were designed and built. According to Rhodes, Oppenheimer said he

couldn't reveal what they would be doing, but he could assure them that their work would end the war and save lives.

The first nuclear weapon deployed in combat weighed approximately 9,700 pounds (4,399 kg) and was 10 feet (3 m) long and 28 inches (71 cm) in diameter. The bomb, named Little Boy, featured a gun-style design with a projectile that, upon striking an interior target, would trigger an explosion. The projectile consisted of nine uranium rings arranged in a hollow cylinder, while the interior target was a solid cylinder of uranium. Four cylindrical silk bags of nitrocellulose powder were placed into the bomb while en route to its target to serve as nuclear gunpowder. A fusing system detonated the bomb after it was dropped and reached an altitude of 1,900 feet (579 m)—a height mathematically determined to have the most destructive effect. At that moment, the uranium projectile launched toward the end of the gun barrel at 980 feet per second (299 meters per second). Ten milliseconds later, the historic and devastating chain reaction occurred over Hiroshima.

Today, in spite of global non-proliferation agreements, nuclear weaponry continues to

haunt us. However, in addition to the threat of atomic bombs, unleashing the power of nuclear fission has also provided us with many incredible benefits, including the commercial use of nuclear power; the Human Genome Project (studying the effects of radiation on reproduction systems); material sciences (designing stronger buildings); nanotechnology; high-speed computing; and the exploration of outer space, which would not have been possible without generators powered by radioactive cesium.

The discovery and application of nuclear fission has moved far beyond weaponry to transform hundreds of industries, including nanotechnology. Miniaturization is constantly being redefined, as seen on this hard drive smaller than the tip of a finger.

> *When you see something that is technically sweet, you go ahead and do it and you argue about what to do about it only after you have had your technical success. That is the way it was with the atomic bomb.*
>
> — **J. ROBERT OPPENHEIMER**

Steam Engine

Without the steam engine, the Industrial Revolution may never have happened. We might still all be out on a farm somewhere, using windmills to grind grain and hitching up horses to bring our goods to market. The steam engine transformed society, spurring manufacturing, creating jobs, and changing the landscape of our world.

Greek mathematician Hero of Alexandria was the first to create a rotating steam turbine wheel, but he regarded it simply as a toy to amuse emperors. Almost two millennia later, steam engines were born from a need to remove water from deep mines. Several inventors, including Thomas Savery and later Thomas Newcomen, tried their hands at creating an efficient method of heating water into steam, which could then apply pressure on a piston and create a recurring motion that would be capable of driving a machine.

Early models were developed with limited success until the engineer and inventor James Watt took on the project. Watt realized that most engines wasted massive amounts of thermal energy by heating a cylinder canister, and he devised a new and more efficient engine. However, Watt did not have the technology or financial backing to develop a prototype. It took almost 11 years and a partnership with Matthew Boulton, who had the money and experience, to see Watt's invention become reality.

In Anna Sproule's biography *James Watt: Master of the Steam Engine,* Boulton's enthusiasm for the project is captured in a letter to Watt: "The people in London, Manchester, and Birmingham are steam mill mad. I don't mean to hurry you, but I think in the course of a month or two, we should determine to take out a patent for certain methods of producing rotative motion." Watt got to work changing the piston's motion to a rotating one, replacing the oscillating motion found in previous models.

By 1775, the Boulton-Watt engine appeared in cotton

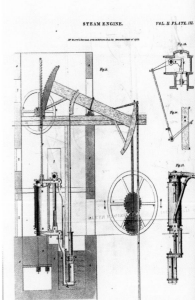

Watt's double steam engine from his specification of 1782.

mills, sawmills, and flour mills, and eventually was adapted to ships, locomotives, and automobiles, replacing the work previously done by horses and men. Fittingly, the steam engine unit of power is called the "watt," designated by the inventor himself and used to determine the functionality of an engine.

Power from the steam engine dominated industry and transportation for 150 years, paving the way for modern machines.

Wastewater Treatment

Wastewater treatment systems are one of those innovations that don't seem all that important until you stop to consider what life would be like without them. What happens after we flush the toilet or run the garbage disposal is not a topic most of us dwell on—one of the many privileges of living in a first-world country.

However, when you compare our way life to that of developing nations struggling with cholera, dysentery, and typhoid fever resulting from the absence of wastewater treatment, it's easy to understand why modern wastewater treatment plants are considered one of the greatest public health inventions of all time.

While gravity-based sewer systems have existed for more than 3,000 years, it has only been within the past century that we have developed widespread solutions to deal with the river of wastewater and its related public health and pollution issues.

Modern wastewater treatment works in three basic steps. In the primary stage, solids are removed from the water and collected for disposal to either a landfill or an incinerator. Usually, this culling process uses metal screens that filter the water into pools, or primary clarifiers, where it sits to allow solids to separate out. Primary treatment is expected to remove about half of the solids, organic materials, and bacteria. At this point, some treatment plants simply chlorinate the remaining water to kill the bacteria, or microbes, before releasing it.

For plants utilizing secondary treatment, the next stage allows the waste stream to flow into oxygenated aeration tanks, where it becomes a concentrated sludge. There, naturally occurring bacteria consume the biosolids, or organic material and existing nutrients. It is expected that 90 percent of all solids and organic materials are removed from the wastewater during this phase.

The last treatment stage uses chemicals or filter beds to remove phosphorus and nitrogen from the water. At this point, chlorine is added to the water to kill any remaining bacteria before it is discharged.

According to the latest UNICEF study on water supply and sanitation, released in early 2013, 36 percent of the world's population—2.5 billion people—lack improved sanitation facilities, and 768 million people still use unsafe drinking water sources.

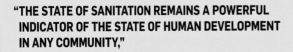

"THE STATE OF SANITATION REMAINS A POWERFUL INDICATOR OF THE STATE OF HUMAN DEVELOPMENT IN ANY COMMUNITY,"

reads a report from the United Nations. It continues:

"Access to sanitation bestows benefits at many levels. Cross-country studies show that the method of disposing of excreta is one of the strongest determinants of child survival: The transition from unimproved to improved sanitation reduces overall child mortality by about a third. Improved sanitation also brings advantages for public health, livelihoods, and dignity—advantages that extend beyond households to entire communities."

Oil Refining

Crude oil pumped from the ground is not pure, and in the unrefined state, it may damage an engine or produce a foul-smelling smoke. An oil refinery converts crude oil into usable gasoline and other petroleum-based products.

The goal of refining is to isolate usable liquids. First, the oil is heated to 662 degrees Fahrenheit (350 degrees Celsius) and sent through a fracking tower, where it becomes cooler as the height increases. As the vaporized oil cools inside the tower, the liquids separate. Kerosene collects at the top, while heavier substances like tar are found at the bottom. After the oil is distilled, pipelines and trucks transport it around the world to consumers who depend on it for innumerable purposes.

Petroleum is thought to have originated from microscopic marine organisms that have been transformed by high temperatures and pressures beneath Earth's crust. The oil and gas migrate through porous rock until they are trapped by impermeable rock. Early miners who discovered the foul-smelling substance saw it as a nuisance and often burned it or deposited it in rivers. But in the 1840s in Pennsylvania, an entrepreneur named Samuel Kier tried to turn the oily byproduct into something of value. Kier's first thought was to use the flammable substance as a light, but it created a lot of smoke and the smell was awful.

He then sought the help of chemist James Booth, and together they developed a simple way of refining petroleum, creating a new type of lamp oil that burned with little smoke or odor.

By the 1860s, there were 58 refineries in Pittsburgh alone. These early refineries used horizontal stills that held five barrels at a time, raising the temperature very slowly. Only concerned with kerosene, they disposed of the rest of the byproducts, like gasoline, for which they had no use at the time.

Today, all compounds in crude oil find uses after refining, but the greatest demand is for gasoline. One barrel of crude oil contains only 25 to 35 percent gasoline, but the demand is so high that oil refineries break down other molecules, in a process called cracking, to make a low-quality gasoline.

The refineries also spit out many other important substances. Asphalt, for instance, is used to pave roads, and fuel oil burns in a furnace to generate heat. Trucks and boats burn diesel fuel. Kerosene becomes jet fuel and supports heating and cooking. Petroleum gas can be used in heating appliances and refrigerants, and lubricating oils, such as motor oil, reduce friction. Paraffin wax insulates buildings, and even bitumen, or tar, is used for paving roads and waterproofing.

In sum, oil enhances nearly every facet of modern life, powering vehicles, creating medicines, forming plastics, and more, all made possible through oil refineries.

Internal Combustion Engine

Did you know that every time you start your car, you create a tiny explosion? That's internal combustion at work. It may sound simple now, but figuring out how to create, contain, and maintain such an explosion required centuries of development.

In 1680, Dutch physicist Christiaan Huygens envisioned an internal combustion (IC) engine fueled with gunpowder. The concept was there, but he never built his design. In 1858, self-taught Belgian chemist and inventor J.J. Étienne Lenoir successfully built and patented the first two-stroke cycle, single-cylinder internal combustion engine with an electric spark ignition fueled by coal gas. The fuel, which he called "illuminating gas," was a mixture of hydrogen, carbon monoxide, methane, carbon dioxide, and nitrogen; it was ignited by an electrical charge from a battery. Lenoir's idea was revolutionary. While many inventors were trying to adapt the popular steam engines of the day for personal transportation, Lenoir had taken a different approach. It worked, although not quite as powerfully as he had hoped.

Since his engines were bulky and inherently stationary, Lenoir manufactured them for power lathes, water pumps, and printing presses, applications well suited to his machines. Reluctant to abandon his dream, however, in 1862 he fitted a three-wheeled carriage with one of his engines, technically creating the first automobile, and drove the vehicle 50 miles (80 km) at a speed of approximately 3 miles per hour (5 kmh).

Several inventors, inspired by Lenoir, took up the challenge and began improving upon his concept—rendering it obsolete. That same year, French engineer Alphonse Beau de Rochas patented a four-stroke IC engine but didn't build the machine. It would be Nikolaus Otto, a German engineer, who claimed that prize. In 1876 he also patented a four-stroke IC engine he dubbed the Otto Cycle that could rival the steam engine for practical use. The reliable power source was an immediate success, and more than 30,000 Otto Cycles were sold in the next 10 years.

German engineer Gottlieb Daimler, who had once worked as a technical director for Otto, designed and built the first prototype of the modern gas IC engine we use today.

Modern internal
combustion engine

1887, Daimler patented the first carburetor,
and two years later he redesigned the four-
stroke engine, using mushroom-shaped valves
instead of the old dome-shaped ones, and
repositioning two cylinders in a V-shape. The
international race to build faster and more
powerful engines had begun—and shows no
sign of slowing down.

Drawing of Lenoir's
internal combustion
engine

Game-Changing Gadgets

CHAPTER **6**

An enlargement of a laser beam illustrates micro particles moving within the beam of light.

Laser

100 INVENTIONS

Science fiction has always had fun with the idea of the laser—think lightsaber duels, Star Trek phaser guns or the ultimate "death ray." The invention of the laser was rooted in these fantasies, creating intrigue and controversy over an invention that, in the last 50 years, has spun off a billion-dollar industry. Thankfully, it has become not a weapon of death, but rather an effective tool that has led to scores of advances in medicine, manufacturing, and even entertainment.

Laser is an acronym, standing for "light amplification by stimulated emission of radiation." A laser can send a single and precise beam of light over long distances. White light, like that produced by a flashlight or lightbulb, actually contains a rainbow of colors that travel at different wavelengths, but lasers emit light that is only a single wavelength. When light travels at the same wavelength, it is less likely to scatter in many directions, which explains why lasers are so precise.

Charles Townes first found success in the maser, which uses a similar acronym as "laser" but instead amplifies microwave radiation. Later, Townes developed similar ideas about visible light and worked with his brother-in-law, Arthur Schawlow, to publish his theory in 1958. An arms race ensued, and Theodore Maiman at the Hughes Aircraft Company created the first working model in 1960. According to the *New York Times*, the first laser shone with the "brilliance of a million suns," but many people thought the new technology was a "solution without a problem." However, in the last 50 years, lasers have been applied to the fields of electronics, law enforcement, medicine, entertainment, and fiber optics, among others. They are also used in precision cutting for paper, wood, textiles, and plastics. Innovators continue to find uses for a direct beam of light, and the scientists who made the discovery have reaped a large reward. Although many scientists have been given credit for discovery of the laser, Nicolay Basov and Aleksandr Prokhorov from the USSR shared the Nobel Prize with Townes in 1964.

LIGHT AMPLIFICATION BY STIMULATED EMISSION OF RADIATION

Transistor

No twentieth-century invention has shaped daily life today more than the transistor. Transistors are the main components of all modern electronics. Without them, there would be no desktop computers, laptops, cellphones, flat-screen TVs, or any of the myriad other electronic gadgets we rely on today. The world would be stuck in a time warp of the early 1940s.

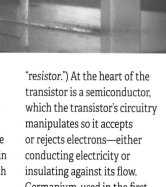

Three scientists—John Bardeen, William Shockley, and Walter Brattain—built the first transistor while working together at New Jersey's Bell Labs in 1947. They were looking for a way to replace vacuum tubes as the main component of electronics, as vacuum tubes took time to warm up, often broke down, and took up a huge amount of space.

The device that Bardeen, Shockley, and Brattain made was composed of germanium (a metallic crystal), gold, and plastic, and was about the size of a human fingernail. Its main function was its ability to both stop the flow of electricity and allow electricity to flow through it on command. (In fact, the word "transistor" is a combination of two other words, "*trans*mitter" and

"*resistor*.") At the heart of the transistor is a semiconductor, which the transistor's circuitry manipulates so it accepts or rejects electrons—either conducting electricity or insulating against its flow. Germanium, used in the first transistor, is a semiconductor. So is silicon, mostly used today.

While the first transistor was the size of a fingernail, the miniaturization of transistors has allowed manufacturers to make electronics smaller and more powerful. Today's electronic chip industry now uses microprocessors (the "brains" of a computer and other "smart" devices) based on a minimum transistor size of 45 nanometers. A nanometer is about the width of three or four atoms—that's some tiny science at work.

For their truly world-changing innovation, Bardeen, Shockley, and Brattain were jointly awarded the Nobel Prize in Physics in 1956.

RFID

Like so many modern technologies, radio frequency identification (RFID) was developed during wartime, when countries wanted to confirm whether the planes their pilots saw on radar were friend or foe. It was Scottish physicist Robert Watson-Watt who invented the first active Identify Friend or Foe system (IFF) for the British. This technology consisted of planting a transmitter on British aircraft, which would receive radio waves from radar stations on the ground, then broadcast a signal in response. RFID works in a similar way, bouncing a signal off a transponder and either reflecting one back or broadcasting a new one.

Since its inception, the technology has been applied to anti-theft systems (the tags that have to be removed or deactivated before you leave the store); tracking systems for nuclear materials during transportation; pet and wildlife location systems; drive-through tolls; payment systems (such as Mobile Speedpass); key cards; and anti-theft systems in cars.

RFID technology uses small chips with an antenna that attaches to a tag. When an RFID reader scans the tag, an electromagnetic field powers up the chip. The powered chip inside the tag then responds by sending its stored data back to the reader in the form of another radio signal.

Over the past decade, as RFID technology has become more affordable, it has also become more prevalent. In 1999, MIT researchers David Brock and Sanjay Sarma gave the world a new way of thinking about RFID applications by developing a system to put inexpensive microchips storing very little data (e.g., serial numbers) on all products and materials within a supply chain. Data associated with the tags would then be stored and accessible via the internet. The networking application allows business partners to understand where goods and supplies are located and when they are shipped and received.

Mark Roberti of the *RFID Journal* believes potential applications for the technology will create safer systems. He says many of the sensors on future airplanes are likely to be RFID-based in order to eliminate electrical wires—and potential fire hazards. In addition, Roberti cites exciting advances in prosthetic technology, diagnostic equipment, and cancer treatment. An RFID-based solution can "offer radiologists a new method for marking a tumor's location prior to surgery," promising "to reduce the risk of infection, while helping surgeons to locate lesions more accurately."

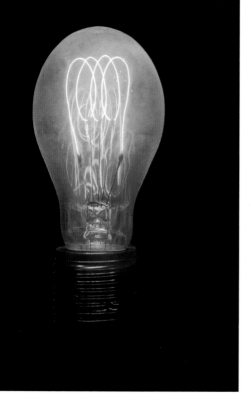

Lightbulb

Today, incandescent lightbulbs have been replaced by even more efficient devices, such as compact fluorescent lights (CFLs) and light-emitting diodes (LEDs). But thanks to Thomas Edison, no one has used candles for everyday lighting since the turn of the nineteenth century.

In 1809 English scientist Humphry Davy created the first light produced from electricity. The arc lamp, as it was called, utilized carbon rods to create a spark. But the lamp had disadvantages: It was too bright and too expensive for general use. In addition, it gave off sparks, making it a fire hazard, especially when used indoors. Over the next century, the technology improved, and the lamps could be found in public places and important buildings, such as lighthouses. Many inventors had small success with adding a vacuum to the bulb or changing the type of filament.

Thomas Edison set up a lab to develop a more efficient and long-lasting lightbulb. In 1879, Edison tinkered with the coating on the carbon filament, as well as the atmosphere inside the bulb, and patented his new lightbulb. According to the Department of Energy, Edison continued to improve his design, eventually using a carbon paper filament inside a vacuum to create new lamps lasting up to 1,200 hours. They became the standard for the next 10 years.

Edison was not the first to create a lightbulb, but his improvement on existing technology brought light into homes and businesses around the world. He was the first to patent the design, and he provided the energy needed to use his invention. He demonstrated that electricity could be distributed from a central generator through wires and tubes.

He also began the first commercial power utility and figured out how to track each customer's electrical use. Consumers of the new technology were connected to a grid of electricity that still exists: Today, almost every household and business is connected to an electric grid. Edison also founded General Electric and Edison-Swan with Joseph Swan, which still dominate the energy world today.

Edison's lightbulb increased the length of the workday, illuminated streets and public squares for safety and longer shopping hours, led to the development of motion pictures, and jump-started the era of energy—prompting the creation of power plants, electric transmission lines, and even electric motors.

INVENTIONS

Zipper

The zipper is such a ubiquitous part of our lives, it's hard to believe there was a time when it wasn't an option. But like most inventions that have become mainstays in daily operations, the small sealing device made up of interlocking teeth was once a revolutionary idea. It has changed the way we dress, improved upon items from outdoor equipment to luggage, and is even used by NASA on space gear.

In 1893, Whitcomb Judson patented the first zipper-like system, which consisted of hooks and eyes along a chain. Known as a clasp locker, it was featured at the 1893 World's Fair. It would be another 20 years before the zipper we know today was developed by an electrical engineer named Gideon Sundback. The patent for his "Separable Fastener" was filed in 1917; Sundback's improvements included adding more fastening elements (or teeth) per inch onto two facing rows of fabric and perfecting the slider that locks the teeth on top of each other. The

B.F. Goodrich Company coined the onomatopoeic term "zipper" when it began designing rubber boots that featured the device.

The first clothing to include zippers in the 1930s was designed for children. The marketing capitalized upon creating independence, and a child's being able to zip up his or her own coat is still recognized as a milestone today. From there, replacing the buttons commonly used on the fly of men's pants was a natural progression.

There are several types of zippers in use today, besides the classic metal type found on jeans and other casual pants. Others are made of plastic, include two slides so they are two-way open-ended, or are concealed behind fabric matching the cloth of the garment. An even more sophisticated system uses coils on each side of the zipper, allowing the slide to wind the coils around each other as it moves along. And then there are even airtight zipper systems, which protect people in scuba gear, hazmat suits, and medical clothing.

Microcontroller

A microcontroller is simply a small computer embedded within another device, but it performs one program or function only and typically uses less energy than a full-size computer.

Microcontrollers were preceded by some revolutionary inventions in the 1940s and '50s. The transistor, which switches and amplifies electronic signals and power utilizing a semiconductor (a substance like silicon, for example, which conducts and controls the flow of electricity), was invented in 1947. This led in 1959 to the development of the microchip, a piece or "chip" of semiconductor material on which millions of transistors and other electronic components form a complete system, or integrated circuit. Then, in 1971, the technology company Intel developed a chip containing a computer-processing unit (CPU)—the world's first microprocessor. From there it was simply a matter of time before all the components of a large computer were integrated on a chip.

Two engineers at Texas Instruments are responsible for inventing the first microcontroller later that same year. Gary Boone and Michael Cochran placed their chip inside a calculator and refined it, ultimately marketing it to the electronics industry just a few years later.

Then, in 1978, the Motorola Company introduced the chip called the Motorola 6801. Like a computer, it contained a CPU; an I/O (input/output) control unit; a timer; RAM; and, because memory was needed to instruct the chip to perform one task only, read-only memory (ROM), which contains information that can only be read and cannot be changed or removed. The Motorola chip was ¼ inch by ¼ inch (6.4 by 6.4 mm). The excitement over the microcontroller and its potential applications, not to mention its relatively low cost of production, led to a flurry of innovation. These early chips were extremely simple and often powered low-energy devices. More sophisticated chips were developed over time to withstand extreme conditions, and while they increased in power, they continued to decrease in size.

Microcontrollers now come with different functions, identified by their number of bits (units of data or information). For example, 4-bit, 8-bit, 16-bit, and 32-bit controllers affect processing speed, size, memory load, and more complex applications.

Microcontrollers help manage many of our everyday functions and are ubiquitous in the developed world. When you are jolted awake by your alarm, brush your teeth with your electric toothbrush, punch numbers into a calculator at work, make labels for your files, use your cell phone, heat up food in the microwave, wash a load of laundry, set your home security system, adjust your thermostat, and click on your TV before bed, you are using a microcontroller.

Furthermore, inexpensive production costs for microcontrollers have sparked a DIY craze in the maker community, where individuals collaborate on groundbreaking electronic and technology ideas. One microcontroller supplier, Arduino, manufactures a line of open-source microcontrollers that you can purchase and apply to a variety of projects, enabling almost anyone with a computer-based idea to begin building a machine from scratch. Many experts believe the future of technology rests in this free exchange of ideas and products.

Optical Sensor

Big Brother may not be watching, but optical sensors increasingly monitor our every move.

Optical proximity sensors are frequently used to enhance a user's experience and to extend battery life on smartphones. For example, if the phone "knows" it is being held up to the user's ear for listening, ambient light sensors will allow the display screen to dim, saving battery power. Optical sensors are also at work when the door to a darkened area, like the inside of a copy machine, is opened, triggering an automatic safety response that halts the operations. Along the same lines, the technology is employed inside factories to monitor production and facilitate automatic safety responses. Optical sensors are also used to monitor the rotating blades on wind turbines and activity on airport landing strips.

Given this ability to measure and react to changes in light, when the sensor "reads" that the available light has increased or decreased, it responds as a photoelectric trigger, either increasing or decreasing the electrical output, depending on the type of sensor.

Today, it would be hard to imagine life without digital cameras, motion detectors, smartphone functionality, and computer features such as the optical mouse, which uses a red LED and an optical sensor instead of the traditional ball-tracking device. The optical mouse is especially efficient for graphic design applications.

When it comes to optical sensor technology, the future looks increasingly bright.

AN OPTICAL SENSOR CONVERTS LIGHT RAYS FROM A LIGHT SOURCE INTO ELECTRONIC SIGNALS. THESE SIGNALS THEN FEED INTO A DEVICE THAT CALCULATES THE PHYSICAL QUANTITY OF LIGHT.

Capacitor

A capacitor stores electrical energy. Unlike a battery, which discharges its load slowly and maintains an even flow of electricity, a capacitor empties its energy in one big burst, firing up a ceiling fan, turning over a car ignition, turning up the amplifier on your sound system, or triggering the flash on a camera.

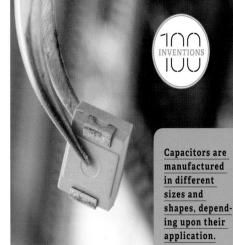

Capacitors are manufactured in different sizes and shapes, depending upon their application.

A capacitor is made up of two terminals, or metal plates, separated by a dielectric, or insulating plate (made of a nonconducting substance like ceramic, Teflon, wax paper, or glass). Once hooked up to electric charges, capacitors receive the current and store that energy on their plates. While plates with a larger surface area can store more energy, it is the dielectric that determines what type of capacitor is needed for a device. For instance, a dielectric like ceramic, a porous material, is ideal in a device that measures humidity, while plastic capacitors and electrolytic capacitors perform best when large voltage loads are needed.

The first capacitor was known as the Leiden jar, named for the University of Leiden in Holland, where it was invented in 1745. The Leiden jar consisted of a glass filled halfway with water, lined with metal foil on the inside and outside, and sealed with a cork. The cork had a metal rod running through it, connected to a chain that hung down to the bottom of the jar. A metal ball at the top of the rod connected to an electrostatic generator, while the outside of the jar was grounded, allowing the inside metal surface to absorb the charge. The equal and opposite charges built up and, when connected by a conductor, gave off a spark of energy.

Benjamin Franklin was fascinated by the Leiden jar, which would prove instrumental to his future experiments with electricity.

Today, most electronics include capacitors. They are vital to touch-screen technology—when your finger makes contact with the screen and passes voltage to it, the capacitor allows for that energy to transmit to the computer. They are especially important in devices that store memory, since when the capacitor is not fully discharged it can act as a temporary battery. This permits your digital camera to retain pictures in memory even when you forget to recharge the battery.

The future of electronics includes supercapacitors—several capacitors strung together that will enable our laptops and phones to recharge in seconds and retain that charge for weeks, even months at a time. Electric cars would also become a more practical alternative to gasoline. Already used in some trains and heavy construction machines, supercapacitors have endless applications.

Telescope

Today, there are two types of telescopes: the refractor and the reflector. In the refractor design, two glass composite lenses—the exterior objective lens and the interior eyepiece lens—work together to draw the light of a distant object into the chamber, bend it to shine on a focus point, and magnify the image for the viewer. Early refractor telescopes used a combination of concave and convex lenses. However, in 1611, German mathematician, astronomer and astrologer Johannes Kepler altered the design to utilize two convex lenses—a tweak that reduced the distortion of images and remains in place today.

In *How Stuff Works*, physicist Craig Freudenrich notes that the reflector telescope functions in a similar way, except instead of an objective lens it uses a "primary mirror" to shine light internally through the aperture onto the magnifying lens. In both cases, the capabilities of the telescope (i.e., how far it can see clearly) depend upon the size of the aperture used to gather light and the magnification capacity of the lenses. The long, tube-shaped body of the telescope acts to position the lenses in correct proportion to each other and prevent dust, moisture, and unwanted light from entering.

In 1990, NASA and the European Space Agency launched the $1.5 billion Hubble Space Telescope into the heavens in order to eliminate the visual interference from Earth's atmosphere. This telescope uses a primary mirror and is a reflector design. The Hubble's most significant discovery to date is believed to be the awareness and increased understanding of "dark energy" in the universe.

"It's generated a tremendous sense of humility because we've discovered how we understand so little about the universe, from dark energy to dark matter to how galaxies can change across 13 billion years of cosmic history," says Space Telescope Science Institute director Matt Mountain. "It's completely changed our perspective on the universe."

Replica of Sir Isaac Newton's first ever reflecting telescope, made in 1668 and now on display at the Royal Society of London.

The hair and glands of a fruit fly viewed through the lens of an electron microscope.

Microscope

The compound microscope, invented by Anton van Leeuwenhoek in the 1600s, was the first big advancement in the pursuit of magnification. The new technology allowed van Leeuwenhoek to make many biological discoveries, including the first sight of bacteria, the details inside a drop of water, and the circulation of blood in capillaries.

The compound microscope contains an eyepiece (with a lens that magnifies to a power of 10 or 15 times) that the user looks through to examine a specimen; objective lenses (which further magnify up to 100 times); an aperture that allows light from an illuminator to reach the specimen; and illumination, usually in the form of a low-wattage bulb. A stage or shelf holds the specimen, and adjustment knobs enable the user to bring the object into focus. Once a specimen is fixed on a slide to the stage, light passes from the aperture through the slide and objective lens and continues through the body of the instrument up to the eyepiece. This invention significantly advanced the field of biology, but its impact was limited by the size of the light's wavelength and the dependability of the light source.

In 1933, German engineer Ernst Ruska conquered these problems with the development of an electron microscope, revolutionizing the field of science. Instead of a light source, a beam of electrons passes through the slide, allowing greater resolution and a more detailed view of a specimen. Electrons that hit the specimen scatter in many directions, while electrons that pass straight on through are captured on the screen below. The discovery earned Ruska a Nobel Prize and transformed our understanding of cell structure and the molecular parts that make up our world.

Electron microscopes are an integral part of many laboratories. There are two types: the transmission electron microscope, which utilizes a camera to send an image to a video monitor (resulting in very high resolution), and the scanning electron microscope, which focuses on a very small part of the sample and enables superior 3-D images.

These microscopes allow scientists to examine microorganisms, molecules, biopsy samples, crystalline structures, and various other surfaces. The technology is also used to produce computer parts, examine evidence found at crime scenes, and search for stress lines in an engine, assisting in a range of disciplines and industries. Modern electron microscopes can magnify objects as much as 300,000 times.

Battery

We depend on them when the lights go out and when we want to change the TV channel. Batteries power modern life in ways big and small, and their evolution continues.

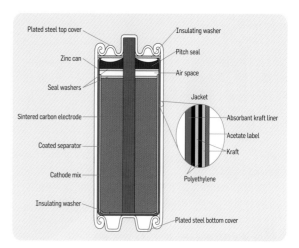

Plated steel top cover
Zinc can
Seal washers
Sintered carbon electrode
Coated separator
Cathode mix
Insulating washer
Insulating washer
Pitch seal
Air space
Jacket
Absorbant kraft liner
Acetate label
Kraft
Polyethylene
Plated steel bottom cover

As legend tells it, the first battery was nothing more than a 5-inch (12.7-cm) clay jar filled with a vinegar solution and designed to hold an iron rod encased in a copper tube. What is now referred to as the Baghdad or Parthian Battery, discovered in Iraq, dates back to the Parthian period 2,000 years ago. If real, the mysterious object could have created several volts of electricity.

Otto von Guericke's 1660 experiments observing static electricity were among the first in modern times to generate a charge on command. Across the pond in 1748, American Benjamin Franklin coined the term "electrical battery" to describe his own experimentation on static electricity, constructing a condenser using two lead plates separated by a flat sheet of glass.

In 1800, physicist Alessandro Volta developed the first voltaic cell. He had discovered that specific fluids would generate a continuous flow of electrical power when used as a conductor and that different elements (e.g., zinc, lead, tin, iron, copper, silver, gold, and carbon) produced varying voltages. He also found that stacking his cells on top of one another increased the output of power. This first wet cell battery, or voltaic pile, was created using alternating discs of zinc and copper with brine-soaked pieces of cardboard sandwiched in between.

Volta's discoveries enabled the production of a continuous stream of electrical current, stimulating worldwide experimentation and development. In 1836, English chemist John F. Daniell refined Volta's concept and produced the Daniell cell, which generated a steady current that could be maintained for a longer time. It was used to power telegraphs, telephones, and doorbells for more than 100 years.

In 1866, French engineer Georges Leclanché brought the evolution of battery technology full circle by patenting a wet cell battery called the Leclanché cell. His design was assembled in a porous pot using rods and chemical mixtures not unlike the earliest so-called batteries from the Parthian period. Leclanché then improved upon the design by substituting ammonium chloride paste for liquid electrolyte and contrived a way to effectively seal the battery.

Although fragile and heavy, Leclanché's zinc carbon cell became the world's first portable battery—and the world has relied on them ever since.

LED Lightbulb

Light-emitting diodes (LEDs) are changing how we light our world in a way we haven't seen since Thomas Edison. Unlike incandescent and fluorescent lightbulbs, which use a filament that can give off heat and burn out easily, LEDs utilize the movement of electrons over a semiconductor to create light. They are very small (less than 1 square millimeter) and emit light in a specific direction. More than five times more efficient than an incandescent bulb, they last up to 100,000 hours. The Department of Energy estimates that 970 million 60-watt incandescent bulbs existing today will soon be replaced by LED lights, conserving a large amount of otherwise wasted energy.

First developed in the 1960s, LEDs were not immediately effective. While working for General Electric, Nick Holonyak Jr. invented the first visible-spectrum LED using red diodes. (A diode is a simple semiconductor that has two terminals that current flows between.) These were valuable in the 1970s as indicator lights and calculator displays, but not for illumination. Soon after, scientists isolated green and yellow diodes, but the elusive blue diode, necessary to create white light, took three decades to perfect. Finally, in the 1990s, two Japanese scientists and one American scientist learned how to produce a blue diode, and the result earned them the 2014 Nobel Prize in Physics.

Because LEDs are so efficient, they can run on cheap, local solar power, bringing light to more than a billion people in the world who don't have access to electricity grids. With the threat of global warming, LEDs can conserve precious resources. Already, LEDs show up in tools we use every day, from traffic lights and flashlights to TVs and smartphones. And as they become more affordable, their presence will be seen in all light fixtures, relegating Edison's lightbulb to the museum for good.

"WITH 20 PERCENT OF THE WORLD'S ELECTRICITY USED FOR LIGHTING, IT'S BEEN CALCULATED THAT OPTIMAL USE OF LED LIGHTING COULD REDUCE THIS TO 4 PERCENT."

— Dr. Frances Saunders, President of the Institute of Physics

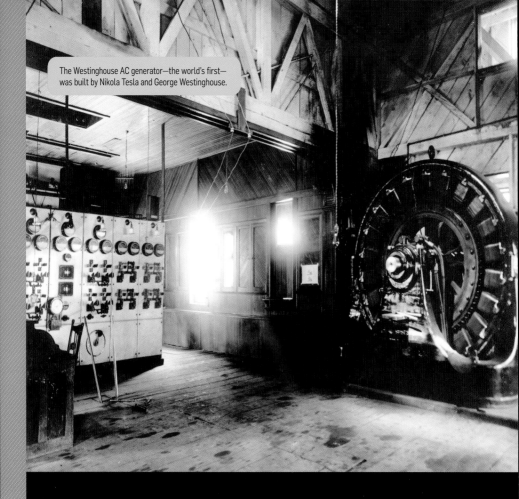

The Westinghouse AC generator—the world's first—was built by Nikola Tesla and George Westinghouse.

The progressive development of man is vitally dependent on invention. It is the most important product of his creative brain. Its ultimate purpose is the complete mastery of mind over the material world, the harnessing of the forces of nature to human needs. This is the difficult task of the inventor who is often misunderstood and unrewarded. But he finds ample compensation in the pleasing exercises of his powers and in the knowledge of being one of that exceptionally privileged class without whom the race would have long ago perished in the bitter struggle against pitiless elements. Speaking for myself, I have already had more than my full measure of this exquisite enjoyment; so much, that for many years my life was little short of continuous rapture.

— NIKOLA TESLA

Alternating Current

In the 1880s, the most popular electrical power source in the world was direct current (DC), championed by American inventor Thomas Edison, but it wasn't the most efficient. DC consisted of a constant stream of electrons flowing in one direction from a positive pole to a negative pole. However, it was difficult to send the desired voltage of direct current long-distance.

Alternating current (AC) operates differently: The charges (also called electrons) move in a constant cycle, flowing in one direction for a short time, then reversing direction, then reversing again. The back-and-forth cycle of switching directions is called *frequency*, and it is measured in hertz (Hz). The more often a current cycles, the higher its frequency. In the United States, the AC frequency is 60 times per second, but that number varies in other countries—hence the need for adapters when you travel.

Croatian-born inventor and electrical engineer Nikola Tesla became obsessed with the concept that AC could power motors more efficiently than DC. In addition, he wanted to solve the problem of how to raise and lower voltage as needed, which was not possible with direct current. Tesla's work led to the invention of the polyphase induction motor, the missing technological link that enabled the long-distance application of AC electrical power and the ability to transmit high voltages with small currents, therefore reducing the amount of heat in the wires.

Today, AC is efficiently transmitted over high-tension power lines with transformers that control voltage, parsing it down from one million to 1,000 volts for general distribution, and then to 120 volts for homes, powering life as we know it.

AC'S ADVANTAGES OVER DC ARE THAT IT REQUIRES THINNER WIRES TO TRANSMIT SMALLER AMOUNTS OF AMPS AT HIGHER VOLTAGES, AND RELEASES LESS HEAT DURING A TRANSMISSION.

For thousands of years, methods of timekeeping were imprecise. Sundials were used to identify the four "tides" of the day, then came large mechanical clocks that relied on a heavy weight—sometimes as much as 1,000 pounds (453 kg)—to turn the gears as it descended slowly during operation. However, since it was difficult to regulate many of the elements affecting the oscillation process (mainly change of temperature and level of friction), the clocks were not reliable and could be off by minutes or hours each day.

Clock

Peter Henlein, a German locksmith from Nuremberg, was responsible for the next technological leap in timekeeping, introducing spring-powered clocks and watches in the early 1500s. Although the method was substantially more user-friendly, the timepieces would slow down as the mainspring unwound and could still be off by hours.

Although some historians credit Henlein as the inventor of the first modern clock, others award the honor to Dutch scientist Christiaan Huygens for his invention of the pendulum clock in 1656, which he patented the following year. Huygens' work is believed to have been inspired by Italian scientist Galileo Galilei, who had studied the motion of pendulums in 1582. A pendulum uses a swinging weight to power its mechanism and relies on gravity to keep it moving. It is reliable due to the property of isochronism, meaning it takes the same amount of time to swing in one direction as it does in the other. The range of motion is determined by the length and weight of the pendulum.

Huygens' clocks were regulated using a mechanism that allowed for naturally occurring oscillation and thus were reliably precise within 10 seconds. It was the first time such accuracy could be maintained. The technology was revolutionary—and our world began to run on time. Inventors spent the next two centuries improving upon the concept and accuracy of the pendulum clock.

In 1927, Canadian telecommunications engineer Warren Marrison developed the first quartz clock. He had been working to discover reliable frequency Standards at Bell Telephone Laboratories when, building upon earlier work in piezoelectricity by W.G. Cady and G.W. Pierce, he developed a clock based on the regular vibrations of a quartz crystal in an electrical circuit.

Marrison realized that the piezoelectric properties of quartz generate a small amount of electricity when placed under mechanical stress. The piezoelectric characteristics also mean that the quartz crystal will vibrate when electricity passes through it. Since all quartz crystals vibrate at the same frequency, meaning they shake the same number of times per second, they are able to maintain a consistent, reliable movement.

In quartz clocks and watches, a battery provides the electrical stimulus to form a circuit with the mineral. The quartz pulses once per second and moves the gears in the clock, or the data on a digital display, accordingly. Barring wear and tear of the casing and mechanical system, quartz timepieces are accurate to within a thousandth of a second.

Gregorian Calendar

We walk around with our calendars at our fingertips, scheduling the days and weeks of our fast-paced lives down to hours and minutes. No matter how hard we work and play, we never seem to have enough time. Imagine a world where time was not reckoned as precisely as it is now. That's the way it was for hundreds of years.

The modern Gregorian calendar, named after Pope Gregory XIII and also called the Western or Christian calendar, is based on a 365-day year divided into 12 months of irregular length. Approximately every four years, the calendar recognizes a "leap year," during which an extra day is added in February.

This method of timekeeping was a shift from the previous Julian calendar (named after Julius Caesar), which had been in use for 1,500 years. The Julian calendar did not accurately reflect a solar year (the time it takes for Earth to revolve once around the sun) and it moved slightly slower than the Gregorian. As a result, an extra day would be erroneously added to the year every 128 years.

Over time, this had the effect of putting the calendar out of sync with astronomical reality. Annual events celebrated on fixed days were slowly drifting through the seasons. In the 16th century, due to the shifting dates, Easter—the most important celebration of the ecclesiastical calendar—was not falling on the first full Moon after the vernal equinox, as set forth by the First Council of Nicaea in 325 C.E.

Italian astronomer, philosopher, and mathematician Luigi Lilio solved the problem. Lilio discovered that the Julian calendar had miscalculated the length of the solar year by 11 minutes. To remedy the situation, Lilio lopped off 11 days from the calendar and introduced the concept of the leap year, adding an extra day in February every four years. Lilio calculated, however, that in order to remain accurate, the occurrence of leap years would also need to be regulated. To remain in alignment, his calendar added leap days in years divisible by four, unless the year is also divisible by 100. However, if the year is also divisible by 400, a leap day will be observed.

In spite of Lilio's recalibration, a discrepancy of several hours has arisen over time. By the year 4904, the Gregorian calendar will be one full day ahead of the solar year—and we may have to refigure time once again.

Mechanical Reaper

Cyrus McCormick's invention started a revolution that changed the world for the better.

The Virginia blacksmith knew his invention was not exactly a new idea. Since humans had first developed farming at the end of the last Ice Age (around 11,000 B.C.E.), crops had to be harvested by hand using scythes and sickles. Doing so was a slow, inefficient, and laborious task, often requiring many farmworkers. And often a crop was destroyed by storms, drought, or insects. Planting was an uncertain profession that drove many farmers to financial ruin.

Roman, Scottish, and American inventors had all attempted to make farming a more reliable enterprise by the mechanization of harvesting—with variable success. Cyrus McCormick's father, Robert McCormick, had spent 20 years working on a harvesting machine. Finally, Cyrus, with the aid of Jo Anderson, a slave held by his family, devised and constructed a mechanical reaper that he felt would work efficiently. In 1834, he received a patent for his invention.

McCormick, of course, wanted to get rich by selling his new machine, but it was slow to catch on even though people were amazed to see it in action. He finally sold seven reapers, all built by hand in the family farm shop. After improving the machine, he received a second patent on January 31, 1845. Still, it took another 20 years before the McCormick reaper gained widespread success and acceptance. By 1872, McCormick was producing reaper-binders, which not only reaped the crop but also bound it into sheaves that could be easily picked up. By 1896, American farmers were using an estimated 400,000 reaper-binders.

"Bank robbing is more of a sure thing than farming,"

It was a cumbersome machine: a platform with two large wheels pulled by a horse across a field of ripe grain. On its side was a mechanized reciprocating knife that cut grain as it came in contact, letting it drop on a platform where it was raked up by a man walking beside the machine.

wrote Canadian author Allan Dare Pearce. Today, reaper-binders have been replaced by giant combine harvesters that perform three separate operations—reaping, threshing, and winnowing—in a single process. Mechanization has enabled farmers all over the world to produce and market food at lower prices, benefiting everyone. And it started with Cyrus McCormick's invention.

Cotton Gin

In 1792, Eli Whitney was a recent Yale graduate looking for a job. What he found instead was a place in the history books. In spite of dreams of becoming a lawyer, he took a position as a tutor on a cotton plantation known as Mulberry Grove in order to repay his debts.

A t the time of his arrival in Georgia, soil exhaustion and oversupply were taking a toll on tobacco profits, and previously profitable farms were in danger of failing. Plantation owners in the Southeast wanted to transition to growing cotton, but they needed to find a way to make it more cost-effective to farm. Separating the sticky green seeds from the cotton boll fibers was tedious, labor-intensive, and time-consuming work. It took the average cotton picker an entire day to clean the seeds from a single pound of cotton.

Whitney's employer, the Revolutionary War widow Catherine Greene, and her plantation manager, Phineas Miller, explained the problem to their new hire and asked if him to help. The son of a farmer, Whitney also had experience as a mechanic. He began working with Greene on the problem. The resulting cotton gin ("gin" being an abbreviation of the word "engine") functioned like a strainer. Picked cotton was loaded into a wooden drum fitted with a series of hooks. When the drum was turned, the hooks snagged the cotton and pulled it through a fine mesh that allowed the fibrous bolls to pass, but not the seeds. Small gins were cranked by hand, while larger machines were powered by horses and later steam engines. The hand-cranked machine was able to remove seeds from 50 pounds (23 kg) of cotton a day.

Whitney was awarded a patent for the cotton gin in 1794. Greene was not credited because, at the time, women weren't allowed to hold patents. The expected financial rewards of the new invention, however, were not forthcoming. Instead of buying cotton gins from Whitney and Greene (or paying the pair to clean their cotton for them), plantation owners copied the idea and

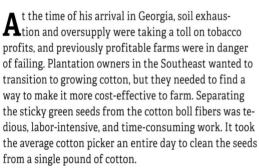

COTTON GIN MODEL, BASED ON WHITNEY'S PATENT DESIGN.

made it themselves—in some cases, reportedly improving on it. Loopholes in patent law at the time rendered the original designers defenseless.

The technology transformed the American economy, allowing cotton to be produced cheaply for both domestic use and foreign sales; cotton became the country's number one export. The invention held unforeseen consequences, however—not all of them positive. Cotton pickers couldn't keep up with the new machine's production capabilities. More hands were needed in the fields, and the demand for slave labor increased exponentially. Whereas in 1790 only six states practiced slavery, by 1860 there were 15.

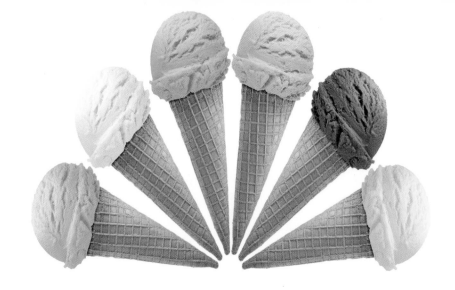

Refrigeration

Want a nice cold drink on a hot day? Your refrigerator works on a simple principle: The cold liquid inside your fridge's coils absorbs heat, which then evaporates into a gas and passes into coils on the outside of the fridge. The gas releases the heat into the room, cools back down, and moves back inside the fridge again to repeat the entire process.

Thanks to this key behavior of matter, getting a cold drink, preserving leftovers, or keeping meat frozen is easy today, but for much of human civilization, all those things were very hard. If you were a rich ancient Roman, for instance, or a medieval king, you could have people cool your drink and food with ice and snow carted down from the mountains. Some wealthy people also had holes dug in the ground which were then lined with wood and straw, and finally packed with snow and ice. This was the only means of refrigeration throughout most of history. People preserved food by fermentation, packing in oil, pickling, salting, and smoking. The problem was that all these methods changed the character, texture, and taste of food. It was generally impossible to keep the food tasting fresh.

The theory that you could build a mechanism that could remove heat from an enclosed space by applying the principles of physics, as in modern refrigeration, was first demonstrated by William Cullen at Scotland's University of Glasgow in 1748. In 1805, Oliver Evans, an American inventor, designed the first refrigeration machine. Jacob Perkins, also an American inventor, built the first practical refrigerator in 1834.

Refrigerators from the late 1800s until 1929 used liquefied toxic gases such as ammonia, methyl chloride, and sulfur dioxide, which sometimes caused death when they leaked out. In 1929, refrigerator makers replaced these gases with the gas Freon, a chlorofluorocarbon, which quickly became the standard for all refrigerators until the 1980s, when it was discovered that leaked Freon damaged Earth's ozone layer. Refrigerators today use refrigerants made from fluorine instead of chlorine that do not harm the ozone layer.

Remote Control

Just imagine having to get up and walk over to the TV in order to change the channel! Sarcasm aside, we have come to rely on remote controls to improve our quality of life at home and work.

Remote controls issue commands from a distance to TVs and other electronic devices such as stereo systems, DVD players, internet radios, and drones. Generally, there are two types of remote controls: infrared (IR) and radio frequency (RF). IR works by sending out pulses of infrared light; RF uses radio waves in much the same way. While most home entertainment components use IR light, garage-door openers, home alarms, and radio-controlled toys are examples of RF remote controls. Unlike IR remotes, RF waves can penetrate walls and go around objects and corners.

In IR remotes, the signal between the handset and the device it controls consists of pulses of infrared light, which is invisible to the human eye but can be seen by a digital camera, video camera, or other device. When a TV watcher, for example, pushes a button on the remote, the handset sends out pulses through a light-emitting diode (LED) that form a pattern unique to that button so the TV knows what to do, such as raise the volume or change the channel. Since IR remote controls use light, they require a direct line of sight to work. The signal, however, can also be reflected by mirrors, just like any other light source.

The earliest use of remote control by radio waves was demonstrated in 1898 by Nikola Tesla. He remotely operated a radio-controlled boat before the public at an electricity exhibition at New York's Madison Square Garden. Tesla called his boat a "teleautomaton." The first remote-controlled model airplane flew in 1932, and remote control technology for military purposes was used extensively during World War II. The first wireless remote technology, Zenith's "Flash-Matic" remote control, which was introduced in 1955 by Zenith engineer Eugene Polley, used light to activate photo cells, turning on a television set and changing channels. But because Polley's remote used visible light, it was often confused by other lights in the room. Infrared devices, which use light to carry signals, came later on, in the late 1970s.

Remote controls now help us start our cars from inside our houses, turn lights on and off, and play music—the applications are endless. Unfortunately, the result is that we are now a population of "couch potatoes."

A staple of popular culture's depiction of cowboys and rednecks, the rifle has a storied place in our social history.

Rifle

A rifle is a shoulder weapon with a steel barrel attached to a handle called the stock. A bullet cartridge gets inserted in the receiver at the opposite end, and the bullets leave via the muzzle. When the trigger is pulled, a spring releases the hammer to strike a firing pin and ignite a powder charge. The energy from the explosion forces the bullet from the chamber.

Firearms were first designed with smoothbore barrels that created very little friction, allowing for high bullet speed but inaccurate aim. In spite of long barrels, their maximum range was 50 to 75 yards (45–69 m).

To imitate the rifling (or angle) of bow-and-arrow feathers, blacksmiths began cutting spiraling grooves on the insides of gun barrels, boosting accuracy and range to 200 to 300 yards (183–274 m). These muskets—further improved with trigger-released, spring-loaded mechanisms that ignited gunpowder using an interior flint striking a steel surface—were called rifles.

Although they provided terrific aim, the guns were not practical in combat. Gunpowder had to be cleaned more frequently from rifle barrels and they were primarily used for hunting. In the 1800s, advancements in manufacturing allowed for uniform mass production and the Baker rifle became the first standard-issue rifle used by the British infantry.

Until 1848, rifle ammunition consisted of soft balls that were pounded into the muzzle with a mallet. This process left soldiers vulnerable during reloading. Then French army officer Claude-Étienne Minié introduced a cone-shaped bullet that could be loaded without a mallet. The new ammunition also proved more accurate and more lethal.

Now, even troops stationed away from the front lines had to protect themselves from far-reaching enemy fire, and the practice of building trenches and fortifications began. By 1863, repeater weapons—rifles that could fire seven shots in 30 seconds—were introduced, with the most famous design being the Spencer carbine.

Flush Toilet

The mechanism is so simple that it is easy to believe flush toilets have always been around. Not so.

Just about everyone has one, and almost everyone has certainly used one. The flush toilet makes modern life more convenient and considerably more sanitary. It works on a simple principle: using the power of water to flush away waste. Toilets consist of a tank holding water connected to a bowl with a seat. Pulling a chain or pressing a handle opens a valve that causes water in the toilet tank to gush into the bowl, sweeping away waste into a sewer or a septic tank through an S-shape pipe designed to keep sewer gases from flowing back into the bathroom. When the bowl is empty, a floating ballcock in the tank closes the valve, and the tank refills under pressure from the water supply.

Flush toilets incorporating a design similar to today's toilets were invented by Sir John Harrington, a writer and a member of Queen Elizabeth I's court. Beginning in the 1770s, a series of inventors improved on the design of Harrington's toilet, leading up to the creation of the first public toilet by Englishman George Jennings in 1851. Jennings installed a number of "Monkey Closets," or toilet rooms, in the Crystal Palace, a cast-iron-and-plate-glass building erected in London to house 14,000 exhibits from around the world.

Enter Thomas Crapper, who founded Thomas Crapper & Company and who promoted the idea of sanitary indoor plumbing. Crapper held three patents for toilet improvements. One story says that "crapper" as a slang term for a bathroom in the United States originated with American servicemen stationed in England during World War I who saw his name on the plumbing and said, "I'm going to the crapper."

The flush toilet may not be one of history's most glamorous inventions, but it certainly has made life infinitely more pleasant. According to *The Economist* magazine, "The flushing toilet still hasn't reached everyone, but it has done billions a great service."

Glossary

Alternating Current (AC) An electric current that reverses its direction at regularly recurring intervals.

capacitor A device that is used to store electrical energy.

condom A sheath commonly of rubber worn over the penis (as to prevent conception or venereal infection during coitus).

daguerreotype An early type of photograph produced on a silver or a silver-covered copper plate (also referring to daguerreotype cameras).

Direct Current (DC) An electric current flowing in one direction only and substantially constant in value.

electrocardiogram The tracing made by an electrocardiograph, which records the changes of electrical potential occurring during the heartbeat. It is used especially in diagnosing abnormalities of heart action.

Gregorian Calendar A calendar introduced in 1582 by Pope Gregory XIII, marked by the suppression of 10 days or, after 1700, 11 days, and having leap years in every year divisible by four with the restriction that centesimal years are leap years only when divisible by 400.

holography The art or process of making or using a hologram.

in vitro fertilization Fertilization of an egg in a laboratory dish or test tube by mixing sperm with eggs surgically removed from an ovary followed by uterine implantation of one or more of the resulting fertilized eggs.

pasteurization Partial sterilization of a substance and especially a liquid (such as milk) at a temperature and for a period of exposure that destroys objectionable organisms without major chemical alteration of the substance.

phonograph An instrument, invented by Thomas Edison, for reproducing sounds by means of the vibration of a stylus or needle following a spiral groove on a revolving disc or cylinder.

radar A device or system consisting usually of a synchronized radio transmitter and receiver that emits radio waves and processes their reflections for display; used especially for detecting and locating objects in space and in the air.

transistor A solid-state electronic device that is used to control the flow of electricity in electronic equipment and usually consists of a small block of a semiconductor (such as germanium) with at least three electrodes.

wind turbine A wind-driven turbine for generating electricity.

Further Information

Bacon, Tony. *Electric Guitars Design and Invention: The Groundbreaking Innovations That Shaped the Modern Instrument.* Backbeat Books, 2017.

Cawthorne, Nigel. *Tesla vs. Edison: The Life-Long Feud that Electrified the World.* New York, NY: Chartwell Books, 2016.

Christensen, Clayton M. *The Innovator's Dilemma: When New Technologies Cause Great Firms to Fail* (Management of Innovation and Change). Boston, MA: Harvard Business Review Press, 2013.

Gallichio, Nicole, and Kevin Anthony Teague. *The Evolution of Meteorology: A Look into the Past, Present, and Future of Weather Forecasting.* Hoboken, NJ: Wiley-Blackwell, 2017.

Harsh, Anurag. *Thinking Tech: Thoughts On the Key Technological Trends of Our Times.* New York, NY: Bookbaby, 2017.

Regan, Sean Michael. *The Total Inventor's Manual: Transforming Your Idea Into a Top-Selling Product* (Popular Science). San Francisco, CA: Weldon Owen-Bonnier Publishing, 2017.

Roland, James. *How Transistors Work* (Connect with Electricity). Minneapolis, MN: Lerner Publications, 2016.

Swaby, Rachel. *Trailblazers: 33 Women in Science Who Changed The World.* New York, NY: Delacorte Books for Young Readers, 2016.

Weightman, Gavin. *Eureka: How Invention Happens.* New Haven, CT: Yale University Press, 2015.

Wooton, David. *The Invention of Science: A New History of the Scientific Revolution.* New York, NY: Harper Perennial, 2015.

Websites

An A-to-Z List of Important Inventions and Innovations

https://www.thoughtco.com/a-to-z-inventors-4140564

This article from ThoughtCo provides a comprehensive list of some of the most significant inventions in human history, along with links to detailed articles on each invention or innovation. The site also provides information on famous inventors and the process of attaining a patent or trademark.

5 Steps for Turning Your Invention Idea Into a Product

https://www.entrepreneur.com/article/77962

This article describes the various factors to keep in mind when inventing a new product, including market demand, the patent process, and the manufacture and distribution of the product.

Inventions: Facts, Figures, Pictures & Stories

http://www.history.com/topics/inventions

The History Channel provides an archive of videos related to historical inventors and inventions, along with links to articles on historically significant inventors and inventions.

Index

100 INVENTIONS